Praise for *Behind the Lights*

"I've known Helen Smallbone for over thirty years and have watched her navigate her journey as a wife and mother of seven with grace and determination. She has been committed to allowing God to order her steps in unconventional yet wholesome ways in order to love her family well and live fearlessly. . . . This book will dare you to be different so you and your children can fulfill your destiny and do greater things than you could ever imagine."

—**Jackie Patillo**, president and executive director of the Gospel Music Association

"Helen is a reflection of strength and relentless perseverance. The story of her life has encouraged me to never stop fighting for my family, my faith, and my joy. Her character is rooted deep in God's truth, and her kindness for others is infectious. *Behind the Lights* reflects her raw authenticity of truth and always choosing what's right over what is easy. You will be challenged in your faith, relationships with others, and living a life above reproach. The world will read *Behind the Lights* and be encouraged to see how Helen walks through hard things and yet comes out looking very different than most do on the other side."

—**Heather Houle,** cofounder of MUMlife

"Make sure you're buckled in, because it was quite a treacherous and miraculous journey as we, the Smallbone family, fumbled our way toward learning how to sing harmoniously in the lights and, even more importantly, behind them. We believe this book tells the story of all the lessons we were taught growing up with heart and courage. *Behind the Lights* truly demonstrates that life is a remarkable adventure."

—**Joel and Luke**, for KING & COUNTRY

"Helen and her entire marvelous family have been dear friends of mine since we first met at the Sydney Opera House for a couple concerts back in the '70s. They're family to my husband Pelle and me! It is a joy to see how God has directed each one of them in life and in music ministry. Jesus has always been the focus, and for that, I salute and thank them."

—**Evie Karlsson**, Dove Award–
winning music artist

"Helen was my first mentor almost twenty years ago, and I have watched her be brave, wise, joyful (that laugh!), trusting in the Lord's provisions, and always prayerful—all behind the scenes. What millions see on stages around the world is possible largely because of the stable and happy home Helen created around the dinner table—even if that dinner table was on a tour bus. I am genuinely delighted for you to get to meet her and learn from her. You'll be inspired to surrender yourself to the amazing adventure God has for you. I know I have been."

—**Heidi Reeves**, mother of three and
mentee of Helen Smallbone

BEHIND THE LIGHTS

BEHIND THE LIGHTS

THE EXTRAORDINARY ADVENTURE OF A MUM AND HER FAMILY

HELEN SMALLBONE

❖ WITH LISA STILWELL ❖

BOOKS

FRANKLIN, TENNESSEE

K-LOVE BOOKS

K-LOVE Books
5700 West Oaks Blvd
Rocklin, CA 95765

Copyright © 2022 Helen Smallbone

All rights reserved. Except as permitted by the US Copyright Act of 1976, no part of this book may be reproduced, distributed, or transmitted without prior written permission from the publisher. For information, please contact emfpublishing@kloveair1.com.

Unless otherwise noted, Scripture quotations are taken from the Holy Bible, New Living Translation. Copyright © 1996, 2004, 2015 by Tyndale House Foundation. Used by permission of Tyndale House Ministries, Carol Stream, Illinois 60188. All rights reserved.

Scripture quotations marked MSG are taken from THE MESSAGE. Copyright © 1993, 2002, 2018 by Eugene H. Peterson. Used by permission of NavPress. All rights reserved. Represented by Tyndale House Publishers, a Division of Tyndale House Ministries.

Scripture quotations marked NIV are taken from the Holy Bible, New International Version®, NIV®. Copyright © 1973, 1978, 1984, 2011 by Biblica, Inc.® Used by permission of Zondervan. All rights reserved worldwide. www.zondervan.com. The "NIV" and "New International Version" are trademarks registered in the United States Patent and Trademark Office by Biblica, Inc.®

Songwriters: Ben Glover / Joel Smallbone / Kyle Rictor / Luke Smallbone / Tedd T
It's Not Over Yet lyrics © Warner Chappell Music, Inc, R1way Music Publishing

Printed in the United States of America.

First edition: 2022
10 9 8 7 6 5 4 3 2

ISBN: 978-1-954201-24-8 (Hardcover)
ISBN: 978-1-954201-25-5 (E-book)
ISBN: 978-1-954201-26-2 (Audiobook)

Publisher's Cataloging-in-Publication data

Names: Smallbone, Helen, author. | Stillwell, Lisa, author.
Title: Behind the lights : the extraordinary adventure of a mum and her family / by Helen Smallbone with Lisa Stilwell.
Description: Franklin, TN: K-LOVE Books, 2022.
Identifiers: ISBN: 978-1-954201-24-8 (hardcover) | 978-1-954201-25-5 (e-book) | 978-1-954201-26-2 (audiobook)
Subjects: LCSH Smallbone, Helen--Family. | Smallbone family. | St. James, Rebecca. | For King & Country (Musical group) | Contemporary Christian musicians--Biography. | Christian living. | BISAC RELIGION / Christian Living / Personal Memoirs
Classification: LCC ML420 .S63 2022 | DDC 782.25092--dc23

Cover and interior design by Dexterity, in partnership with Brain Design and PerfecType.
Cover photo by Mitchell Schleper.

To the legacy given us by our parents:
Geoff and Jean Francis
Jim and Betty Smallbone

"The greatest legacy one can pass on to one's
children and grandchildren is not money . . .
but rather a legacy of character and faith."
—Billy Graham

Contents

Contents

Foreword

Prayer hugs to calm my nerves before going onstage as a teenager. Talks about anything and everything while sitting on Mum and Dad's bed. Folding washing, doing dishes, cleaning houses together. Asking for parenting advice in the kitchen at the farm during a drop-in visit. Watching Mum in the role of grandmother to my children. The thousands of memories I have of the woman who wrote this book are priceless! Prepare to be blessed and inspired by her—like she has blessed and inspired me. But before you embark on her remarkable journey, I'd like to say a few thoughts about my mother, thoughts that hopefully give you extra insight into who she is.

My mum is real. This book reads like Mum is sitting in her living room sharing her story with you over a cup of tea. This is truly who she is. After being "second mum" in our family and her "right hand," I feel like I can read Mum very well—like a book, actually. I love that *Behind the Lights* invites you to read her heart, our story, in such an authentic way. Reading parts of our journey in this book brought me to tears as memories came to mind that I haven't thought about in decades. Our story has never been documented like this before now, and the fact that Mum has shared so honestly and authentically speaks to the true person. You are reading *her*.

My mum is servant-hearted. On family holidays when the family gathers, she is in the kitchen for hours, cooking, preparing a tasty meal for the family she loves. I'm not sure how she is available for all of us seven grown kids when we need her for advice, grandbaby-sitting, or care of any sort, but she is. She has sown faithfully into her family, and now, in recent years, into other moms' lives and their families. She has passionately poured herself into Mom to Mom meetings, then MUMlife, and now the masses with her podcast through AccessMore. She has viewed each as a privilege to serve, and her energy for it comes from purpose—her God-given mission.

My mum is faithful. My dad cries pretty much every time he talks about Mum. I know that it is largely because of how faithfully she has loved him. When he was broken and at his most emotionally fragile after huge setbacks and worldly rejection, she did not doubt him or waver; she did not fear for the future of our family of nine. She knew God would provide and that Dad would come through. That belief was used to bring our family to the season we are in today—a season of much fruit from that faithful trust.

My mum is wise. I cannot count the number of times I have called her asking for her thoughts on all sorts of topics to do with parenting, faith, and family life. I now have her on my K-LOVE podcast regularly, too, as I love giving my audience a chance to glean from her hard-earned wisdom. If she doesn't know what to advise, she will say so and ask for a bit of time to think and pray about it. Often we will pray about my question then and there. (See? Wisdom.)

My mum is humble. She is the kind of mom who has said that she's been "quite happy" for her kids to be the ones in the spotlight and not her. She says it with a sparkle in her eye and in all sincerity. She knows the challenges of having a profile and truly has enjoyed the view as a support person. Which is in large part why I sense God has entrusted her with this book—He loves humility. He blesses humility. And my mum is strong, but humble. Thank you, Jesus, for such a woman, with a message for such a time as this. A woman who has a passion to encourage women, mothers, families.

I'm not sure that I could have had a better example of a true Proverbs 31 kind of woman. One of the biggest goals of her life has been to see her children "arise and call her blessed" (Proverbs 31:28 NIV). On Mum's sixtieth birthday, we "kids" rented a house as a family, had a beautiful meal together, and did just that: each in our own way paid tribute to her and called her blessed. So, in this moment, Mum, I say thank you. Thank you for loving Jesus first. Thank you for loving Dad faithfully and well.

Thank you for raising us the way you did—in the love and truth of Jesus. I pray that this book will bless God's people and bring much fruit for His kingdom and glory. You are treasured, Mum, and I arise and call you *blessed*.

Rebecca St. James
November 2021

Introduction

I confess I'm my happiest when I'm behind the scenes—I have spent my life in the background—but there I was, lit up onstage with my husband, David; Joel and his wife, Moriah; and Rebecca, who was emceeing. Luke would have been there, too, but he was recovering from vocal surgery. It was June 12, 2021—the night before the K-LOVE Fan Awards—when AccessMore put on "An Evening with the Smallbones." There were a couple of thousand people in the audience who wanted a more up-close look into our musical family, sometimes referred to as the Australian von Trapps. Some have even likened us to that of a farmer's family or a circus family in that the children have grown up as a vital part of the business. We have been a touring family for the past twenty-seven years, with much of it in the spotlight in some way or another.

It was a very sweet night, and we had some fun laughs and meaningful discussion that, I think, gave a glimpse into some of our family's dynamics. Then, when our time was over, and with the cameras that were filming for the public turned off, Joel addressed the audience. He announced that he and Luke had been writing a new album, and they wanted to premiere a song they had written for me called "Unsung Hero."

In that moment I was very grateful I had previously heard the song. They'd played it for me on Mother's Day, and I could tell then that Joel and Luke were both very proud of the piece and keen to see my reaction. I knew it was written from a deep place and was being presented to me as a thank-you gift for being their mum. It was an honor I wholeheartedly accepted—not only for my years of hard work but for all those fellow mothers out there who pour their hearts into their families. Deep down, I believe *every* mum is an unsung hero.

As Joel introduced the song to the audience, I realized our son Ben had put together a video to go with the song—a video I had not seen on Mother's Day. There were photos and videos of my parents; of David and me when we were dating; of us when we were married; and photos of the kids when they were small, right on up to Luke's wedding day and for KING & COUNTRY performing onstage. By the time it was over, there was not a dry eye in the place. It was all so very precious, and watching it quickly took me back and flooded my mind with the journey God has brought me on from my childhood in Australia where I grew up to our family farm in Tennessee where David and I live now.

It's been quite a journey, filled with the testing and growing of my faith and God leading us all step by step toward living "outside the box." I never thought my life would unfold the way God has led it. Living outside the box is countercultural and has, without question, been a different path from the way the world says we are supposed to live. There is a certain expectation from the world about what life should look like. It is expected that we are to graduate from high school, go to college, and get a job that takes us from 8:00 a.m. to 5:00 p.m. five days a week. "Normal" people should prepare for retirement, have medical and life insurance, get married, and buy a house. We are supposed to set goals and, when we reach them, get awards and nice vacations. At my age—now sixty-six—we are supposed to retire and attend to our bucket list.

We as Christians do this as well—we often create our own agendas and goals, then attach God's name to them. We ask Him to bless our plans and efforts to live out what we want.

After we left Australia, we were forced outside the box of normal, as you will see. It is not a journey I would have chosen to live, but I would not change anything about it. It led us to following God in ways I would not have thought possible. We have lived in the extraordinary, where we have had to rely on God to provide and where we have seen His hand actively working in and around us.

Part of the reason I wanted to write this book is to encourage and challenge other families to live differently—to get out of their box. I want others to have courage to seek His will rather than their own and to let Him use them however He wants in His bigger plan. His plans don't look like the world's definition of success, but they always include lasting, eternal purpose and value. They also include His presence, leading and guiding us into adventures and valleys we wouldn't necessarily choose for ourselves. Through them, I believe God wants more of us living counterculture to the world's ways. Sometimes it may even mean we go against a lot of the church's "religious" traditions. But in choosing His ways, we will live in the miraculous!

I look back on my family's journey, and I see God's hand everywhere. I see His phenomena. I see His faithfulness in taking our simple Australian family and leading us to the other side of the world and doing things with us we would never have thought possible. Our lives are a living testimony of believing God's promises and trusting His timing and His ways—even when circumstances didn't make sense and were not easy. He was always there.

Our journey has been an amazing one we never would have planned for ourselves. There has been a lot of loss— at one point we lost everything—yet God has redeemed every one of those losses beyond what we could have hoped for or imagined, which is why Ephesians 3:20 is one of my favorite verses: "Now all glory to God, who is able, through his mighty power at work within us, to accomplish infinitely more than we might ask or think."

This book is a look back from this mum's viewpoint of my own family's transformation from living more in the world's way into God's way. It's filled with life lessons that, hopefully, you can apply to your own life and to your own journey. David and the kids would have their own perspectives, perhaps slightly different from mine, but I can only speak from what my experiences have been and the memories they bring—some good and some not so good. In some small ways, I wish I could go back and do some things differently, which I'll touch on. But in most ways, I wouldn't change a thing. What we've been through is what makes us who we are today and molds us into the instruments God has wanted us to be for bringing Him the glory in our lives that He deserves.

What is exciting to me is I know and fully believe that the faithfulness and favor God has shown me—shown all of us—is the same faithfulness He shows to anyone who fully commits their life to Him. It is my hope that from our story, you will be inspired to step outside of your box and embrace God's plans for you without fear or hesitation. When you do, His peace will carry you no matter what you face, the same way it has carried me.

PART ONE

IN THE BEGINNING

CHAPTER ONE

FROM HEAD TO HEART: A STRONG FOUNDATION

I will ask the Father, and he will give you
another Advocate, who will never
leave you. He is the Holy Spirit, who leads into
all truth. The world cannot receive him,
because it isn't looking for him and doesn't
recognize him. But you know him,
because he lives with you now and later will be in you.
John 14:16–17

As I've come across people over the years, many are amazed at my family's story. Our ministry and musical outreach have been so large for so long, spanning the life careers of Rebecca St. James and for KING & COUNTRY. There's a surprise from others about how these two entities came out of one family and curiosity about how we all came to be who and what we are today.

They want to know how it is we've worked and stayed together through obstacles and detours most "normal" families don't encounter.

There isn't one response I can think to give. Our journey has been filled with a variety of faith-stretching occurrences that could only have been orchestrated by God, both in their inceptions and in His miraculous outcomes. But for me, as a mum who loves Jesus, I am convinced that nothing we have accomplished or overcome would have happened without His divine intervention and our commitment to follow His lead, regardless of how unusual or against the flow His plan seemed.

I'm also convinced that a person won't realize the incredible magnitude of what God has in store for them unless they are all-in in their relationship with Him.

With that, I'm very intrigued with the interaction between the dual inputs of our head and our heart and the decisions we make. By that, I mean that sometimes we learn things through our head knowledge without experiencing them in our heart.

I realized this when I was growing up as a Methodist minister's kid. I grew up in the church and was involved in church and Sunday school every week. At the time, we lived on one of the busiest street corners on the northern side of Sydney in a quaint English-style parsonage next to a beautiful, historic stone church in Chatswood. It was expected that my brothers and I would be actively involved in my dad's ministry. At times we were his secretaries answering the phone, and I knew and often interacted with the church staff.

It was there in 1968—at thirteen years old—that I went forward at a Billy Graham crusade. After listening to him, I realized I had never actually made my own decision to accept Jesus as my Lord and Savior, and I was ready.

Looking back, I know now that it was a decision I made with my head, and it changed my life. For the first time, I had an incredible thirst for reading my Bible and acquiring knowledge about God—something I had not done before. I also had a deep hope that my strained relationship with my mum would heal. I was the youngest and only girl, with three older brothers.

My mum told the story that, after she gave birth, the doctor said, "It's a girl."

Mum then said to the doctor in amazement, "Are you *sure* it's a *girl*?"

And he said, "Yeah, I can tell the difference between a boy and a girl!"

The problem was that as I grew up, she wanted me to dress in feminine styles and do indoor things that girls traditionally did back then. But I wanted to be one of the boys.

Before moving to Sydney, we had lived in a small town in rural New South Wales where there was room enough to roam. I loved being outdoors with the dogs and chickens and playing games with my brothers. Sometimes I'd even take off on my bike with a friend and be gone all day without anyone else knowing where I was. So there was a constant underlying tension between my mum and me, and I was all too glad for my dad's sweet, kind, and fun demeanor that acted as a buffer.

By the time I turned fifteen, things changed for my family. Mum, who was quite energetic, took off on a foot race with my brothers down a hill and slipped a vertebra in her back so that it began pressing on her nerves. She had to go onto bed rest for three months. It was a difficult season because, at the same time, my dad was getting discouraged in the ministry. He had a strong, simple faith, and I admired him for his love for people and his humble belief in who Jesus is. But he wasn't seeing the Holy Spirit working—people weren't coming to Christ. Plus he was growing tired of the continual drain of being a pastor.

It was then that my mum's doctor, who was a Christian and attended our church, told her and Dad about a faith healer coming to town, and he wondered if she might be open to going. So they did. Mum went forward for prayer, and God touched her in a very real way. The next morning, she was able to sit in church for the first time in three months! She didn't receive complete physical healing all at once, but there was a noticed improvement that brought her hope and continued healing as time passed. Even more, she and my dad experienced a spiritual change that opened up both of my parents to the charismatic movement and the outpouring of the Holy Spirit that occurred in Australia in the early 1970s.

Eventually, they brought all of us kids to the gathering, and it was then that I went forward once again—this time to receive the Holy Spirit—and experienced an encounter with Jesus I'd never felt before. My faith went from the head decision I'd made the year before to a full-on heart decision. I knew then that I had the Holy Spirit inside of me, just as His Word says He will do if we ask Him (John 14:16–17).

It was completely transformative—and it was the beginning of seeing my mum in a whole new light. I began talking with her and Dad on a deeper level, and Mum and I were finally able to begin repairing and healing the years of strain and brokenness, for which I am so thankful.

Dad also changed and developed a renewed passion for Jesus. Over the next year we continued to become more involved with the charismatic movement and watched it transform the church. Dad was seeing more conversions and believers having an added excitement about their faith. My brothers and I got very involved in the youth ministry, and for the first time I saw the Holy Spirit literally fill a room with His presence. I saw His Spirit break down the hardness of hearts, convict us to repent, and cause an outward expression of joy that only His forgiveness will bring.

It was revival. It was also when I met David.

* * *

A pastor's salary back then was not very high, and with four kids to feed, it was normal for Mum and Dad to take in boarders for the extra income and to help some needy young man. Besides, what was having one more young man around when they already had three sons? Needless to say, it wasn't uncommon for us to have an extra face at the dinner table.

Well, one Sunday night after the church service ended, I went straight home to change into my pajamas. Mum eventually came home and said, "Gosh, there's a nice young man I talked to at church tonight, so I asked him to go to the coffee hour afterward." That was where all the young people hung out after church.

Then she said, "It would be good for you to go over there too."

I said, "Eh . . . okay," and got out of my pajamas and dressed again. Then I randomly took our galah (a rose-breasted cockatoo) named Charlie out of its cage, put him on my shoulder, and left. I have no idea where my thinking was, but I guess that since I thought I *could* take the bird with me, I *would*!

I walked over to the gathering place, and as I was about to enter, the young man Mum had met walked out. He could not walk straight past me. After all, I had a galah on my shoulder.

He said, "Oh, you're Helen!"

"Yes, how did you know?"

He went on to explain how he'd seen me in church and then seen some photos of the youth group with names and ages on the wall in the coffeehouse, and he recognized me in one.

Well, I was intrigued by his attention to detail, so we stood outside on the porch and talked for five or ten minutes, at which point David asked if I was only sixteen.

"Oh, no, I'm seventeen now!"

The entire time, Charlie sat on my shoulder, and I think David thought it was absolutely hysterical.

After that night, my mum invited David to a family outing and learned he was unhappy with where he was living. She also learned he came from a good family in Brisbane, so she invited him to live in our caravan (the Australian term for *camper*) that sat outside the parsonage. We were planning to relocate in three months to a new church about twenty minutes away, and she said, "You know, he's a nice young chap, and I feel sorry for him. If after three months it doesn't work out, I'll just say 'We're moving! See ya!' and that way nobody's feelings will get hurt."

Well, he moved in.

In the meantime, Mum saw how well we got along—we talked every time we could, whether on the porch, in the yard, on the phone, wherever. She told David that since I was still a seventeen-year-old schoolgirl and he was twenty-one, there could be no relationship with me, and she said as much to me about him.

* * *

As David and I got to know each other, we were amazed at all we had in common and the similarities between our families. I came with three older brothers, the oldest named David. David also came from a family with three boys and a girl that was the youngest, and he, too, was the oldest. We both had dogs named Chip. And years later, I found out that when David discovered his mum was pregnant with her fourth child, he even suggested she name the baby Helen if it was a girl.

My dad was a Methodist minister, and David's dad was a Methodist lay preacher but bank manager by profession. My parents were strong in the Temperance Union—meaning clean living, no cards, no dancing, etc. David's grandmother and mum were the stalwarts in their town for the temperance movement. Both of our families moved regularly, so we both came from rotating, insecure lifestyles compared to most other families.

It was crazy, all the similar nuances and understanding we shared about each other's lives. Through it all, we became very close friends, and deep down, I knew I liked him. But there was one thing that held me back: David wasn't serious about Jesus. He had the head knowledge but not the heart relationship I had. Being that that was more important to me than anything, I decided against a close relationship. I knew it wouldn't go anywhere in the long run.

In the meantime, the three-month trial period of living in our caravan went by quite quickly, and my parents decided to invite David to join us when we moved to another Sydney suburb called Turramurra. Dad started ministering at their new church in the beginning of 1972. Since David was not where I needed him to be spiritually for me to have a serious relationship with him, I thought I would keep my eye out for other eligible young men. For me, a new church meant a new beginning.

It was not long after moving that I met a young man who was the current youth leader at the new church. Bob was serious about Jesus, and we established a closer relationship over the next few months. Then one night at a Bible study and prayer time we held at the parsonage, David attended and sincerely asked for prayer. He knew he hadn't been walking with Jesus—he was walking on the edge of a relationship with Him. He wanted what we all had. He saw that our faith was alive and real, and he wanted it too. So we prayed for him.

Not long after, Bob quickly figured out that he and I were no more! I was a bit embarrassed, but there was no ignoring that the Holy Spirit had definitely ignited the element I had been missing in David. He became very active in youth outreach, we renewed our friendship, and when I was twenty and David twenty-five, Dad married us. It was all really very sweet. I married my best friend, and afterward, David liked to quip, "We lived together before we got married, but we didn't sleep together!"

* * *

Looking at our story, I say with complete sincerity how very important I think it is to have more similarities of background than not with the person you marry. It's vital to be equally yoked and to share the Holy Spirit, not only in ministry but in daily living and in prayer together. Your similarities affect how you relate, they affect the level of understanding in how the other thinks, and they help to build a strong foundation as you grow and work through tough times as well as your successes together.

With that being said, even though David and I genuinely enjoyed each other's company, we didn't know just how vital our spiritual and relational backdrop would be for the series of events to come—events that would catapult us out of normal, traditional ways of living into adventures that would stretch our faith beyond our wildest imagination.

CHAPTER TWO

SO *THIS* IS
MARRIED LIFE?

Love is patient and kind. Love is not jealous or boastful
or proud or rude. It does not demand its own way. It is
not irritable, and it keeps no record of being wronged. It
does not rejoice about injustice but rejoices whenever the
truth wins out. Love never gives up, never loses faith, is
always hopeful, and endures through every circumstance.
1 Corinthians 13:4–7

It's not uncommon for newly married couples to begin
life together on a high note, but then eventually comes
the realization that things are playing out differently from
the way you thought they would. The plans and visions
in a new bride's mind become clouded and, before you
know it, those exciting visions fade. I was no exception
to this phenomenon. Yes, David and I knew each other
really well and had a strong bond together, but the reality

of living a traditional lifestyle had its challenges for me during our first years together.

After we got married, we lived in a small house in Sydney. I had graduated from occupational therapy school and began working at a nursing home while David worked for a small record company. But this thing of working eight to five plus commuting forty minutes each way was foreign to me, and it was a hard adjustment. As I've said, I grew up in a parsonage where my family was always around. Dad had appointments and commitments, but he stayed mostly in the general area and was accessible a lot of the time. And with my mum home full-time, our family was a close community—we were together more than we were apart. So the adjustment to my and David's reality was sobering.

We'd both come home in the evenings, and I would say, "So how was your job? How was your day?"

Then he'd look at me frankly and say, "You know, I just want to forget about it and simply enjoy being home."

So, I'd start talking about my world, which involved therapy for old people—I know, not the most exciting topic!—and I could tell he wasn't even listening. I thought, *So* this *is marriage? It's really not all it's cracked up to be.* You give your best hours out there, you come home exhausted, and you basically go to bed and do it all again day after day. It did not gel with me very well, and I thought, *This is not really living.* You marry a person because you love them and want to spend the rest of your life with them, and yet you hardly spend any quality or quantity time with them.

I began to feel very alone, even somewhat abandoned, as time went on.

To make things even harder, my parents became concerned about David not being present enough, and they started to nag about it, which didn't help. Even though I understood their concern—even agreed with it to an extent—I began to feel defensive on David's behalf. This added tension on top of tension, especially, once again, with my mum.

In the meantime, David had his own vocational and spiritual awakenings to maneuver.

* * *

David grew up in Queensland in rural areas, but eventually his family ended up in Brisbane. He never went to college, but he began working at a young age and over time discovered his natural talents and took jobs that allowed him to use them. At the age of sixteen, he started playing double bass and singing harmonies with some mates in local after-church coffee shops. It didn't take him long to realize his own musical limitations and that his real love was booking gigs, organizing equipment, and helping in whatever way he could. The members of the band he was in changed, and David ended up managing his brother, Ian, and two other brothers—Phil and Ian Truscott—in a

Christian harmony band called Family. They honed their skills in coffee shops and churches.

After David finished high school, he worked as trainee manager for a small department store—and hated it. Then he worked as a cameraman for a local TV station but was retrenched—or laid off—during an economic downturn. In desperation, he went for an interview for a position at Paul Hamlyn Publishing. He was so desperate, he said to HR, "If you hire me for this position, you don't need to pay me for six weeks. You won't regret hiring me, as I will do a great job."

He got the job *and* the pay. And he did so well that they promoted him to national sales manager of book-stalls in department stores, and at the age of twenty-one he moved to Sydney. After a few lonely months in the big city, he happened to find himself driving fairly regularly by a quaint, historic stone Methodist church in the suburb of Chatswood to visit a then girlfriend. As he sat at the traffic light on the road beside the church, he would say to himself, "I need to go to that church sometime." He made that visit in August 1971 and sat at the Sunday-evening service behind my mother, my brother and his fiancée, and me. The rest is history.

* * *

David worked very hard at Paul Hamlyn, putting in long hours, and during the first year he managed to double the sales of the previous year. However, they kept raising the bar for him to produce greater sales while putting out lower-quality products, and it became very frustrating and difficult to maintain the pace. He continued working long hours, but he could no longer reach their sales quotas. Eventually, he quit.

His next position was with a small music magazine publication—but only for a short time. While selling ads for the magazine, he met an executive named Ron Hurst who worked for a mainstream record company called M7 Records. Ron offered him a job as promotions manager. This is where David worked when we got married.

At the record company, David marketed and promoted some of the biggest names in Australian pop and country music in the seventies. He also ended up getting Family (his brother's group) signed to M7 Records. Family's first album went gold, which was a significant achievement in that day. They also had a single titled "Hallelujah Day" chart on Top 40 radio.

But even though he loved promoting his brother's group, David struggled with the other artists on the M7 roster. He would see them display one behavior onstage, then see who they really were offstage, and it bothered him. Many of the artists were role models for kids, but they didn't live the roles they portrayed. It really disillusioned him to be using his marketing and promotional skills without a purpose greater than himself.

Between his internal struggle and about a year of my parents' continued nagging about the amount of time David focused on work, I resigned from my job at the nursing home, and we moved closer to his family in Brisbane, Queensland. David's parents didn't criticize, make demands, or even speak into our lives, which was a huge relief. We could just *be*, and it was nice.

David took a new job in marketing and promotion for a local radio station called 4BK, which seemed promising. By then he had developed a well-rounded experience in media. Between TV, marketing his brothers and folk groups in coffee shops, overseeing sales and marketing in book publishing, promoting top stars at a record company, and now radio, his confidence was building. But the longer he worked at 4BK, the more he realized deep down they also played music that had nothing to offer people. It all still felt *empty*. He wanted his life to count; he wanted it to mean something. He wanted to really live more for Christ.

In his search for a vocation that had a greater, more eternal purpose, we decided to move back to Sydney in 1977, with me about seven months pregnant with our eldest child, Rebecca. To help, my mum came up to assist us in packing, but while I appreciated the gesture, it didn't take long before her nagging about David started all over again. One day I finally reached my limits and lost it. I turned to her and said, "Shut up! We have lived for the last year without any expectations or criticism, and here we haven't even gotten back to Sydney yet, and you're already criticizing my husband. I warn you—you keep this up, and I will have to choose between you or my husband, and I know who I am going to choose!"

She burst into tears and went to her room, and I sat there stunned at myself. I had never spoken to my mum like that before. And I never used the words *shut up*.

When David came home, I told him what had happened. We didn't see Mum the rest of the night. As we lay in bed, we listened to her crying through the night, and I also shed some tears—of remorse for losing my temper and of doubt about our return to Sydney and what it might mean for our lives.

That occasion was so momentous, I don't even remember the rest of Mum's trip with us, but I do know that it lived on in our relationship. Mum and Dad never criticized David again—and trust me, they had the opportunity. We all acted as though nothing had ever happened, but out of hurt, David shrank from them. We all still visited one another and were civil, but David's attitude was tainted by the fear that they weren't really interested in him—they only wanted to see me and the children—and he would often retreat during visits, to be found in a room by himself reading or sleeping.

Even though tensions eventually settled down, I was learning the reality that when two people get married, they not only marry their spouse, but they marry into each other's entire families, and there *will* be conflict. Even with the most well-intentioned acts, boundaries are tested, and feelings get hurt. Balancing where your parents end and your marriage begins can be a two-steps-forward, one-step-back journey, but looking back, I know now that there can be progress. Especially when there's forgiveness and grace—something David and I eventually learned.

* * *

Once we got back to Sydney, David set up his own company. He named it Rhema, which means "spoken or living Word," and started working with the members of Family. They were passionate twentysomethings who were somewhat unskilled yet had big dreams. They quickly set up a record label as well as a distribution label.

With Family involved, it was natural to do Christian concerts across Australia. One of the first tours that Rhema promoted was a Larry Norman concert with Family as the support artist. David dreamed big on that one and filled the Sydney Opera House. By then, I had just had Rebecca, and this was the first concert she ever attended. She was six weeks old.

Rhema grew quickly as the Christian industry emerged during that era. David had large, fancy offices in downtown Sydney—and the overhead to go with them. He worked all the time, but I will say it really wasn't work to him. It was more like an all-consuming desire. In a way, his dreams were bigger than his common sense. He was impassioned about setting up Christian music in Australia and bringing in artists from all over, so he began doing Australia-wide concert promotions. He also opened a Christian bookstore and published a Christian music magazine. He was a pioneer in the Christian industry in many forms and had found his path—making a difference in people's lives through music.

Over the next four years David scheduled local concerts for Family, as well as toured international Christian artists such as Keith Green, Leon Patillo, Phil Keaggy, Randy Stonehill, Andraé Crouch, Chuck Girard, Dan Peek, and the Korean Children's Choir in conjunction with World Vision.

Now, when it came to concert tours, there's one thing I need to point out in order to provide a clear picture. Australia is similar in size to North America—without Alaska and Hawaii—and in the early eighties there were probably all of twenty million people who lived there. To give perspective, there are about the same number of people living in New York alone. So while there were millions in population, there was also great distance between the major cities with not a lot going on in between. Planning and touring the artists to all the major cities took a *lot* of work, with long hours every day. And at the same time David was working hard growing Rhema, I was working hard with a growing family. Rebecca was a toddler when Daniel was born in 1979, and then Ben came along in 1981.

* * *

Back in the day, we didn't have cell phones or instant messaging. There was no texting or tracking apps. There was only a landline and nothing else. Communicating took much more effort then than it does today, so oftentimes, the kids would be in bed before David got home, without any communication between them during the day. I thought it was pretty rough on them. I remember feeling a weight of grief that they didn't see him much. Of course, I didn't see him much either. I remember not even knowing what to do with his meal each night. Or mine, for that matter. I could eat dinner with the kids, but that didn't feel right—I wanted to eat with him. Sometimes I'd hold off eating for when he came home, but I often didn't know when that would be. I'd call him at six fifteen to find out an arrival time, and he'd say, "I'm just fixing up one last thing, then I'll leave." So in my mind, he'd be home by seven fifteen or seven thirty. A little after seven I'd start reheating our meals on the stove (we didn't have microwaves then either), and by seven forty-five when he still wasn't home, I'd think, *Do I wait? Do I eat?* By then I'd be starving and take his meal off the stove and go ahead and eat mine. Then I'd reheat his again when he got home. A lot of times, he came home to a pretty angry wife.

Finally, one night when he came home late yet again, I broke. I was *furious*, and when he walked in—I slapped him across the face. He just stood there, looked at me, and said, "Don't you ever do that to me again."

And he walked out.

He left for about two hours, and I was an absolute blubbering mess the whole time. I desperately wanted to be heard by him—things were at a very serious point for me—but I realized that getting him angry was *not* the way to address it.

When he came home, he was obviously upset, but my anger had turned into absolute remorse. I never did it again, and I know now that his response of leaving was the wisest thing he probably could have done. After that incident, I tried to understand more of his side and where he was coming from, but it remained a continual frustration.

I share this story because I understand that all married couples have one problem or another, no matter how close they are, and if the Helen I am today could advise the Helen I was back then, it would be to pray—pray about *everything*. Philippians 4:6 says, "Don't worry about anything; instead, pray about everything. Tell God what you need, and thank him for all he has done." It's so important to pour your heart out to God and turn to Him for the comfort you need or the solution you're looking for. He hears and He cares about all of it, and He *will* bring an answer. But more than anything, no matter how good a friend you may be with your spouse—the way David and I were and still are so close—they can't possibly fill every single void you find yourself in. There is only One who can do that, and it is God Himself.

* * *

Well, as God would have it, David continued to put in long days planning and touring artists to all the major cities, and the workload became an increasing challenge for him, especially with his additional load of the bookstore, the magazine, the record company, and a distribution company. In time, he became spread very thin, and while it had already affected our relationship, it now also affected relations with his partners. In addition, there was the problem of always being undercapitalized and growing too quickly in a small market (only about 5 percent of Australia's then twenty million population were committed Christians). Something had to give, and in 1981, with Ben a babe in arms, David was asked to step down.

At the beginning of 1982 he left, and Rhema quickly went downhill and found itself insolvent very fast. They simply didn't have David's passion or direction to keep going. But after he left, God answered my years of praying for an opportunity to be together more and live day to day in the community I so longed for.

CHAPTER THREE

THREE CLOSED DOORS

Even when the way goes through Death Valley,
I'm not afraid when you walk at my side.
Psalm 23:4 MSG

After Rhema ended, David remained undeterred. He knew that part of the problem had been the high overheads and being spread out in too many areas. He had also realized his real loves and wanted to focus more on them: live concerts and recording music that would live on in peoples' hearts. So he set up another concert promotions company, but this time on his own, and he decided to keep it small. He'd learned from his mistakes and wanted to approach things differently. He called the company David Smallbone Promotions and started a record company called DTS (David Thomas Smallbone) Records.

David set up this new company in the living room of our small home, and, for me, it was like a homecoming!

He was available, he was around, I could hear and know what was going on. I felt *so* much more a part of his life. The sense of community I had been missing had finally returned, and I was elated. There was a simplicity in being able to put the kids down for a nap and have the freedom to run to the grocery shop. Sometimes I'd come home, and David would be holding a baby while working, but he didn't mind or resent any of it. He loved family life, and he loved the children. The new setup was an answer to prayer, and it all felt so right.

A few years later—about 1983—we moved from our tiny home into one that was a little larger and had a separate sunroom for when people came over to work with David. We also had a garage that we used to store albums, cassettes, and promotional materials, so it worked better for our needs all around. And it was during this time and in this space that the kids and I began sitting in the living room and packing mailouts together. At David's and my direction, little hands worked away at stuffing envelopes and licking and putting on stamps. It was very much a family affair—everyone had a job, everyone had a purpose. We didn't know it yet, but it was also the inception of our learning to work together on a much grander scale in the years to come.

* * *

In 1984 Joel was born, and we dreamed about our family's future. We would often go on Sunday-afternoon drives, and even though at times the kids would whinge, "Why do we have to go for a drive?" the time together would invariably turn out to be good. One Sunday we drove into the northern suburbs of Sydney, and David said in his dreamy way, "I think we need a place that's a little bigger. I don't want to go back to an office scenario, but we need a house that has maybe a small warehouse with it."

As he spoke, I looked out my car window and saw a For Sale sign in front of a cute ranch-style house. What really got my attention, though, was the warehouse behind it that was as big as the house. I exclaimed, "Wow! Look! That one's for sale!" God worked in His mysterious ways, and we ended up buying it.

The new house was larger than our previous homes and sat on five acres where the kids had space to run and play. There was even a tractor, which David loved driving. It had two living areas with one already set up as an office, and then there was that huge warehouse in the back for storage. It felt like our first *real* family home to me and as though it was meant to be.

After the move, David's business continued to do very well. He promoted the biggest names in Christian music such as Stryper, Whiteheart, Petra, Resurrection

Band, Bryan Duncan, Carman, Larry Norman, and David Meece. Then our son Luke joined us in 1986. Luke loved growing up on the property. His favorite thing to do was to go on the tractor with David.

And, to add to all the goodness that was happening, the relationship between us and my mum and dad had improved. They were a big support with the birth of each new baby, and they were helpful with home projects. Each new development was such a blessing to our young family.

With each successive child joining the family, we all continued to accompany David to the concerts that were in or close to Sydney, in places such as Newcastle and Wollongong. Sometimes he would take one of the kids with him to Brisbane since his family lived there. He found great comfort in us being with him, and we did too. Since we all helped with the mailouts and putting flyers on cars and other jobs, I think it was good for the kids to see the fruition of the work they'd been doing at home. It all came together so well.

When we traveled, I'd bring sleeping bags and whatever else we needed, depending on where we stayed, which was either the Sydney Opera House or another facility called the Hordern Pavilion. If we stayed at the Opera House, I'd choose a dressing room for us to stay in, but if we had to stay at Hordern, it was a different setup. The dressing rooms there were very old and dirty—too dirty for me to let my children lie down on the floors. I was usually pretty flexible, but I still had my standards, especially where the kids were concerned. So, if we stayed at the Hordern, we'd bring our big German shepherd cross, and . . . with what I'm about to say next, I'd probably get into trouble with Child Protective Services today, but when it was time for bed, we'd park our van at the back door of the building where our dressing room was and put the kids in bed in the van with the dog. There was no way anyone would try to get in the van with him there! And David and I would periodically go out and check on them to make sure all was well, which it usually was. It's certainly not something we'd do today—everything's so different now—but we did what we had to do to make it work in those days.

* * *

By 1988 David had brought just about every Christian singer or band from the States to Australia except for one major artist he still really wanted to host. So he put in a good offer for a tour . . . and succeeded. This particular artist had toured Australia before but with other promoters. In preparing for a tour David would project concert attendance and expenses and set up a budget before agreeing to an artist coming and before signing a contract. On this particular tour he budgeted for similar attendance numbers to the previous concerts but due to unforeseen circumstances the Australian audience did not show support as they had in the past. Attendance for the tour actually came in 40 percent lower. This meant a devastating loss of about $250,000.

We had incurred some losses in the past but could balance it with other successful concerts. We knew this was going to be different, and we were not going to be able to carry this shortfall.

I remember so well sitting in our dressing room and hearing the news. Our room was right next to the tour manager and his team, and I heard David say to them, "We're down. We're down 40 percent, and I'm going to lose my shirt on this one."

The hard part for me—and this impacted David to the core—was listening to my husband ask, "Can you reduce my payment at all, 'cause I'm gonna lose everything?" They just laughed and said, "Hey, man, we have lived up to our side of the bargain. You signed the contract!"

For me to sit and hear this, from my perspective on the outside, hearing that verbal exchange—not just their rejection of his request but their laughter and uncaring tone—was very hard. To this day, I tear up when I think about it.

It was closed door #1.

* * *

At the time all of this was unfolding, Josh was born, and David was about to turn forty. Between dealing with such a dilemma and now having six kids, we began going through some significant changes, unaware there was about to be yet another setback . . .

David had been seeing the starts of what God was doing in the churches in Australia with their praise-and-worship music, especially at Hills Christian Life Center where we attended. David thought their music was so good that it needed to be available to a wider audience than just the local church, so he convinced them through a handshake deal to let him record an album, market and promote it through DTS Records, and see what happened. It went well, so they did another album, which also went well. But by then the church had realized he was on to something, and they decided to take over the recordings at the church and not have David involved.

The day they told David the news was the same day I had planned a big surprise fortieth birthday party for him. I got his mum and dad to come down from Brisbane, I got one of his best mates and his wife to come from Adelaide, and there ended up being about twenty-five people there. Everyone hid their cars in the warehouse out back so he wouldn't suspect anything, then we all gathered in the living room and waited for him to come home.

Well, after all of David's meetings that day, including the blow of Hills CLC not wishing to work with him anymore, you can imagine his state of mind as he walked in and saw the living room full of his family yelling

"Surprise!" He went white as a sheet. He literally had to sit down. One extreme collided with the opposite extreme within a matter of seconds, and he struggled to get his head around it.

It was closed door #2.

* * *

By now, we knew we had to go through with selling our home to pay off some of our debt, downsize, and make some major life changes, so we moved to Brisbane, which is less expensive to live in. Plus David's family was there. We rented a tiny three-bedroom home where David and I had a full mattress in one bedroom, the four boys slept in the second bedroom—side by side on mattresses on the floor because there wasn't enough room for beds—and the third bedroom had Rebecca on a single bed and a crib for Josh. There was a little backyard where the kids could play, and we just made it work. I actually enjoyed our time there, because even though it had been a very hard year for David and me, we were heartened to see that our life changes were still beneficial for the kids.

In the meantime, we encouraged my mum and dad to move to Brisbane, too, so we could all be together. And that's when David really took to the project of finding them a house. He went out of his way to help them, and they were very touched, and because of his efforts, true healing began to take place. They sold their home and moved to a place only about a mile away, which is the closest we'd ever lived to one another. Families from both sides were all together, and the kids got to see their cousins and be with all the grandparents on a regular basis.

We enrolled the kids in a Christian school where two of my brothers taught and a bunch of cousins attended, and from my perspective, it was a pretty good year going forward. Rebecca loved to sing, so she got involved in the school's music program. They had a rock band consisting of older, more senior kids, but even though she was only thirteen years old, she decided to audition anyway. And she got in! When the guy who ran the program heard her, he made some recordings of her singing songs he had written, and this encouraged her a lot.

The timing of this, of course, was God's hand on her and on us, because by then, 1991 had rocked up, and David was planning a national tour with Carman.

* * *

David had done quite a few tours with Carman before. He'd even come up with an arrangement to set up a record and promotions company just for him that was similar to what he had done so successfully with Hills CLC. It would have meant moving us all to the States, so in the latter part of the previous year, David and I had taken Josh, who was only a year old at the time, and flown to Carman's home in Oklahoma. Our goal was to cement plans for David to work with his management team on the details and to check out schools and housing.

We stayed with Carman's mother, and I must have cried every day while we were there over the strangeness I felt. I had never seen so much "religiosity" before—which felt so superficial to me compared to the more authentic faith I was used to. It was mind-blowing to this simple Australian girl. I think the final straw for me was the Sunday evening we went to church, and they didn't want Josh with me in the back of the sanctuary—they wanted him in the nursery. He was very quiet, but being a one-year-old, it was hard for him to sit still, so naturally I let him down so he could walk between David and me. When an usher walked up and said, "I'm sorry, he's gonna have to leave," I said, "Okay, he leaves, we leave." The irony for David and me was that the name of the church was Grace Church.

Afterward, I looked at David and said, "I don't know what's gonna happen, but this is a lot for me to take. This whole thing doesn't feel right."

The problem was, with two closed doors behind us, David felt strongly that he couldn't keep doing Christian music in Australia. He had verbalized to me that if he kept on doing what he was doing in Australia, he would die young, as it was too much stress and there weren't many other alternatives. The door with Carman was a door God had opened, and we couldn't walk away. So we kept proceeding with plans to make the move, and Carman proceeded with his plans to do another tour in Australia in February 1991.

When Carman arrived, he was glad to see the kids. He had been around them numerous times and enjoyed their nuances—he got along especially well with Rebecca. As it turned out, in Australia, when an international artist comes over, they have to include a local support act in their show in order to protect the Australian music industry. Carman didn't perform with a support artist, and he did not want one, so David told him about Rebecca's involvement in the Christian rock band at school and suggested putting her onstage. She could do three praise-and-worship songs, and that would satisfy the Australian musicians' union. Plus it would be fun. Carman agreed, and David began grooming Rebecca for performing and touring. Every afternoon after school the two of them would walk to a small local church and use their hall to practice her three songs on a stage using tracks.

Then they hit the road. While they were touring, Carman bought and gave David plane tickets for the whole family to come to the US after the tour; he was all in and ready to move forward with their business plans. But when they arrived in Adelaide, the pastor of the church where Carman was to perform—someone David had worked with before—got in Carman's ear and said, "You know, Smallbone's a failure. He just lost everything. Why would you want to associate your name with his?"

Those words played on Carman's mind, and when he went back to America, he called David just days before Easter weekend and said, "David, I just don't think this is gonna work."

David was shell-shocked.

It was closed door #3.

PART TWO

AMERICA, THE FIRST YEARS

CHAPTER FOUR

ONE — AND *ONLY* ONE — OPEN DOOR

For I am about to do something new.
See, I have already begun! Do you not see it?
I will make a pathway through the wilderness.
I will create rivers in the dry wasteland.
—Isaiah 43:19

So, there we were with a third door closed on David's work, and he was absolutely devastated. With each door that had shut, he'd thought he still had one more opportunity. But now he knew he had nothing. He was reeling with emotions about what to do next and said, "I can't keep doing Christian music here, but I don't know anything else! I'm not interested in something like real estate, as your mother suggested, or promoting secular music. It's not in my heart—I would die."

Knowing David as I did, I knew he was right. He *would* die trying to do anything else—the Christian music industry was his calling. But it was hard to know what to do and have a clear mind after all that had happened.

It was Thursday of Easter week when David came to me and said, "I have to get away for a few days." So we packed the kids up and hopped into our van and headed up the Sunshine Coast about one and a half hours north of Brisbane. Easter is a very popular time to get away, though, and with no internet and it being a last-minute decision, we did not know where we were going to find accommodations.

As we drove, David and the kids scoured the road-sides to find any place that did not have a No Vacancy sign. Every time we would stop, David and our eldest son, Daniel, would jump out of the car and check, only to come back to the car feeling a little more deflated. Daniel finally ended up saying, "When I grow up and I have a family, I am never doing this to them!" (The amusing thing is he is now grown and has a family of his own, and he remembers this incident and says he would totally do this to his family. Funny how life changes us!)

Well, eventually we ended up in a beach town called Noosa (Noosa is the ritzy area of the Sunshine Coast) and it had just started to rain. We pulled into another block of units at the end of Hastings Street, and both of them hopped out again. But this time they came back with smiles on their faces. We had found a place! With sleepy, tired kids we climbed the incline up the side of the hill and found our unit. It was very nice, and had the price tag to go with it, but desperate times make for desperate measures. We knew it was only for the night, and the next day we'd be on the move for a more affordable place, but in that darkest hour, God gave us fresh hope and joy not only with such a beautiful place to stay but with a new blessing in the conception of our youngest child!

* * *

After having a little time to think about what to do, David wrestled with the thought of going to America in spite of the closed door with Carman. We still had the plane tickets. Carman had wanted them back, but after talking and praying about it, we said no, we were keeping them. By then, we had sold our house and most of our furniture in preparing for moving to the States and had taken the kids out of their school. We'd been living in a holding pattern for the upcoming, dramatic life change, so we viewed the tickets as a nonrefundable deposit and thought it was the least Carman could do for us. So we held onto them until we were certain about what to do next.

I asked David if there were any other opportunities in America he might have—he had promoted a lot of other people from there too. After pondering it, he thought it might work if we just looked at going to the States for two years. He suggested he go first to see what he could set up; he didn't want to take the rest of us unless he had something lined up. So in June David flew to Nashville and got David Meece to hire him as his associate manager. We had promoted him very successfully in the past, so there was already a good relationship. They agreed on a salary, Meece connected David with a Realtor to help us find a house, and it looked as though God was indeed still leading us to America and opening a new opportunity!

Before we all left, David had thought about it and decided to make a recording of Rebecca singing Australian praise-and-worship songs to take with us. Being only fourteen, she had handled the tour with Carman well and demonstrated an ability to keep her head together through it all. David wanted to see if he could market her in the States after we got there. In the meantime, we whittled down the rest of our belongings to fit into sixteen suitcases (we were allowed to bring two cases each, and that was it).

I also knew I was pregnant with Libby by then, and given all the healing and how close I had become with my mum, it was a very hard conversation to have. To tell her and Dad I was expecting another baby and leaving the country in one sentence was not easy. But they didn't complain or try to stop us. They sensed God was going before us. They at least knew there were no other real options for us in Australia.

On August 24, 1991, we said our final goodbyes and flew to Hawaii.

* * *

The immigration officer eyed the eight of us, then took a good look at our sixteen suitcases and said, "Hmmm . . . What sort of visa are you on?"

He directed David into an office with a window where I could see him and the officer could see us, and we knew we were flagged. We had a six-month business visa, so he was trying to figure out why there were so many of us and why we were so loaded with luggage. He didn't think we looked as though we were only there for vacation or business.

At that point, Rebecca started crying. I lowered my head to her and said in a whisper, "Rebecca, you shut those tears off straight away. We are a family who is coming over here for an extended vacation, so you just cut it out." Then I sucked in my tummy, thinking they didn't need to see or even wonder that I was pregnant.

After more talking and explaining, however, the officers couldn't find a sound reason for holding us any longer, and after about an hour they finally let us through. We all heaved a sigh of relief!

Once we landed in Los Angeles, we drove down to San Diego to stay with some Australian friends for a week while we contemplated how we were going to get to Nashville. We had such a nice time with them, but how they put up with all of us, I'm not sure! They are our friends to this day, but I still think about all they did for us and how they let us stay with them an entire week. Honestly, we needed all the encouragement we could get from them.

We couldn't afford to fly us all to Nashville, so we decided to take the train. Since we couldn't get a sleeper car and would have to sit up the whole time, we did it in increments. We rode one leg to Albuquerque and got off for the night to sleep and clean up at a hotel. Then we rode to Kansas City and spent one night there. The plan was to then take a local connector train to Carbondale, Illinois, where we'd connect to another larger train going down to Memphis from Chicago.

At one point while we rode the dinky connector train, it came to a complete stop in the middle of nowhere. We thought, *What in the* world *is going on?* David left to find the conductor. We were horrified to find the train had run over a homeless person that was walking along the tracks, and we all had to wait for the coroner to come! The kids thought it was great, but I thought it was a pretty crazy introduction to America. Little did I know what would happen next . . .

By the time we got to Carbondale to change trains, it was ten o'clock at night, and we had missed our connection. We were told we'd have to take a taxi to race to catch it at the next stop. Well, it doesn't take much thought to realize we couldn't fit the eight of us and sixteen suitcases in one taxi—the train company had to hire an Astro for us and a regular cab for the bags! But we got to the next station around 1:00 a.m. and were very relieved that the train was still there waiting for us.

The problem then was that they had given our seats away since we had missed the connection, so we had to separate and take whatever we could get. The conductor was very apologetic, but there was nothing he could do. So Rebecca got a seat in between two guys at the front of the carriage where two rows faced each other. Daniel and Ben sat together next to someone who smoked, which they were uncomfortable with. And David, Luke, Josh, and I sat together with Joel across the aisle. I felt fortunate that we were at least all on the same carriage.

We were all exhausted by then, and I couldn't help but feel sad but amused as I watched Bec fall asleep on a guy's shoulder with her feet up on the people facing her. They'd put her feet down and she'd bring them back up . . . then they'd put them back down . . . all while she slept. It was all a bit surreal in so many ways.

We finally made it to Memphis at five o'clock in the morning. After we unloaded from the train, we were all ready to sleep in real beds and decided that even though we only had one more leg to get to Nashville, we wanted to spend a night in Memphis. But getting to a hotel presented the same issue with transportation that we'd had at the last train stop: too much baggage and too many kids for one cab. We talked to a driver about our options. There weren't any vans—at least not at that time of the morning. I said, "Can we leave the baggage at the station and all of us fit into your car?"

He looked at his five-seater car and back at me and said, "I could lose my license!"

Well, we didn't know what else to do, so he reluctantly let us pile in and hoped for the best. I stuffed the smaller kids on the floor in the back and the older ones sat crammed on the seats. Fortunately, we didn't have very far to go.

The next morning, we were able to get another Astro, but it was still too small; we had to pile luggage on the roof. Packing it was a master enterprise, but we eventually got everything and everyone in place and made it to Nashville.

The whole trip really was quite the experience, and some people might look at this part of my story and cringe, but I don't. I remember how David had previously joked that I married him for adventure, and I think that is definitely true. I don't mind things being a little up in the air and spontaneous. I actually prefer that than for daily life to be predictable. I suppose that ties in with not liking the whole nine-to-five job scenario and going on the same vacation every year. It's not my mentality, so there's truth in saying I love adventure. That's a good thing, considering all we had just gone through up to that point.

I've been asked what it was like to leave our family, our country, the culture we grew up and lived in. Well,

I didn't feel in the least that I was leaving in defeat. In fact, I felt quite the opposite—I felt as though we were all stepping into hope. It was clear that God closed doors He could have kept open. He had taken everything from us. He took away every back door. He took away every "out" there was. The only thing we had were the plane tickets, and we had to keep moving forward. Sometimes God puts us in situations where all we can do is go through the circumstances He allows or even leads us into. I equate it with the Israelites facing the Red Sea. If they had turned back, they would have died.

David was also very vulnerable in those days. He felt like a failure. I sometimes think about what our life might look like if I had not supported him. If I had stopped believing in him. What if I had not practiced submission in our home? What if I had not understood that David, under God, was and is the head of our home? I trusted that God was leading us even though our life at that stage was very unpredictable and uncertain.

An even bigger question is, What if I had trusted David instead of God? I think I would have pointed out David's failures. I think I would have spoken harsh words or criticized him. And if I had done that, he would have curled up and died. Not literally, but inside.

If you were to liken the family to a ship, I think the role of the wife is that of the rudder. The rudder is small in comparison to the size and strength of the ship, and its

47

work is unseen as it guides the ship in a certain direction, so a wife holds tremendous power in her marriage and in her family. She has the power to crush or the power to bring life. Her role and attitude often set the tone for how decisions are made and what direction the family goes. If I had put my hope in David rather than God, we might never have left Australia. We would never have seen the plans that God had for us. Jeremiah 29:11 says, "'For I know the plans I have for you,' says the LORD. 'They are plans for good and not for disaster, to give you a future and a hope.'" If I had trusted David over God, we wouldn't have seen the miracles God has worked in our lives since that time.

What we had were God and each other. We each clung tightly to God while looking for His hand . . . His leadership . . . His guidance. And we clung tightly to each other for support and encouragement we couldn't have gotten from anyone else.

It was hope that led us here, and it was hope that led us forward into a new day, into a new adventure.

CHAPTER FIVE

NASHVILLE, NEW BEGINNINGS, AND THE GOODNESS OF GOD

The LORD will guide you continually,
giving you water when you are dry
and restoring your strength.
You will be like a well-watered garden,
like an ever-flowing spring.
Isaiah 58:11

Driving into downtown Nashville was surreal. It had been a couple of weeks since we'd left Australia, and it was a relief and *so* nice to know we were finally at our destination. There were many unknown details, but I still felt an element of excitement to see how this new adventure would play out. God was still encouraging our spirits with hope.

We knew we needed a place to stay while we looked for a house, so David called a manager friend who lived in Nashville who had some sort of deal with Union Station Hotel in downtown Nashville. He told us to go there, mention his name, and they'd set us up, so we did. They gave us a basement suite that had three rooms—a bedroom with a king bed, another room with two queens, and a small adjoining living area with a pullout couch. Even though there were eight of us and I was then five and a half months pregnant, I thought we were doing alright and couldn't help but feel grateful for God's provision. I could see how He had gone before us to make such a space available. Having those three rooms was a game changer for my spirit.

We stayed there for a week, and sometimes having all the kids together in one space for that long was a challenge. There were times they'd all play in the room with the two queen beds, and when somebody squealed, I'd stand in the doorway and say, "I don't care what you do, just don't break anything!" then shut the door. I remember them making forts between the beds and using the beds as trampolines. As we had done in the past, we made it work.

Breakfast at the Station was free, so in the mornings, we'd all wrap up, go to the dining area, and eat all we possibly could. There were no grocery shops in the area, but we were lucky to find a pharmacy, so for lunch we'd get a loaf of bread and simple stuff like peanut butter. Then for dinner we'd go to McDonald's. That was the routine, and by later in the week, I said to David, "I just can't look at another hamburger. I can't look at another piece of bread. I need something that's better than this."

Well, during our stay we did a lot of walking and visiting free places (our favorites were the capitol and the Tennessee State Museum) and that evening we decided it would be fun to go for a free trolley ride around town while we figured out what to do for dinner. After it drove some blocks away and made a big circle around Music Row, the trolley headed back toward the hotel. And that's when I saw a sign in front of a restaurant that read Kids Eat Free on Wednesday Night. I blurted, "Wait! *This* is Wednesday night!" So with excitement we all got off and went in. David and I had the salad bar, and the kids ate free, and for fifteen dollars we had a really good meal.

I remember thinking how wonderful it is when you have a real need, and then you see God meet it. He truly knows us and wants to give us what we need. Between the trolley ride and the free meals, it was incredibly special. The way He provided made us all feel very cared for and that He was with us. At the end of the day, that is all you need.

* * *

Our days at Union Station were spent with David connecting with people he knew and letting them know he was in town. Then, when we weren't trying to figure out where the kids could play or what to eat, he wanted me to go with the Realtor David Meece recommended to look at some rental properties. So while David stayed with the kids, I went with her to look at homes.

One thing I noticed in all the areas we looked was that there were no trains or buses for public transportation. We didn't have a car, and I didn't know when we'd get one, so that was something I wasn't sure how we'd handle.

After looking at four homes that were all very similar, I finally said, "If you had a family, which area would you live in?" She said she'd definitely go with the older estate in Brentwood we had looked at—it sat on one acre. I said, "Okay. Let's do it."

The listing agent for the house we chose said he didn't normally do rentals but was doing a friend a favor. She'd told the guy that we moved here from Australia, we had no furniture, we had six kids, and that I was pregnant.

"Oh, *seriously?*" he said.

"Yeah!" she replied.

And so, on September 17, one week after arriving at Nashville, we excitedly moved into our rental in Brentwood. The house was completely bare of any extras except for a fridge and a single mattress the owner had left because he said he could not live with himself having a woman who was pregnant sleeping on the floor. The house also had a big backyard. I was thrilled to finally be "home," for the kids to have a backyard to play in, and for our new life to begin.

Our new dilemma now was that we were miles from any grocery shop, and we had no car. Meece said that when he was out of town, which was frequent, we could drive his car, so that worked for a bit. He also had an old dining room table and four chairs that he let us have.

At the end of our street sat a local public school, and David asked if we were going to enroll the kids there, but I was very hesitant as school had already started, and with us being in a new country, I frankly could not have emotionally handled not having the kids with me. So I told him I planned to homeschool for at least the first year (I had already begun homeschooling before we left Australia), and we'd reassess after that.

To survive the coming weeks and months, David and I treated our circumstances with gratitude and as though everything was normal. We all began praying together each day for God to provide and leaning on our trust in Him that He would come through. Each morning before we started school, we would gather together in the living room, sit on the floor, and pray—for our daily needs and for God to provide for our bigger needs.

While we waited for His provision, I made beds for the kids by tucking the sheets I had brought with us in and around their winter clothes, and I put a sweater in each pillowcase for their pillow. The kids thought it was a lot of fun—a bit like camping but in a house. They weren't upset or worried at all about not having real beds. They also loved playing cricket with a plastic bat and ball in the empty living room, so they thought it was an adventure.

For doing laundry, I would throw their dirty clothes in the bathtub after everyone had had their bath and let them soak overnight. In the mornings I would squeeze everything out and hang each piece outside on twine to dry. This worked fine through the rest of September and October, since the weather was warmer and the clothes were thinner, but I knew that by November we'd need the heavier clothes they were sleeping on since the weather would get colder. I wasn't sure what I'd do, but for the time being, things were working out.

David began working with Meece, plus he started shopping Bec's music. He wanted to see if anyone was at all interested in joining the praise-and-worship movement that was taking off in Australia—he was pretty keen on bringing it to America, starting with Rebecca.

After meeting with one local producer named Greg Nelson, Greg said, "Why don't you let me and my wife take you and Helen out to dinner?"

So we went, and afterward I invited them over to the house to meet the family and have a cup of tea. When we rocked up and walked into an empty living room and a dining table with four chairs, he said, "Wow! You guys okay?"

I said, "Yeah! You know, we're having quite the fun. This is just like camping, only in a house! The kids get to play cricket in the living room—they've never had an entire living room to do whatever they want in—so they think it's grand!"

Well, evidently, after Greg and his wife left, they went home and talked about it, then went to their church the next Sunday and rallied their Sunday school class. Not long after that, we got a knock on the door, and maybe half a dozen people came in and started walking through the house. We didn't even invite them in. They just walked in and began writing stuff down on paper. We weren't sure *what* they were doing. As some of them chatted with us, the others kept walking around. And then they finally left.

A few days later, we got another knock on the door, and the same people were there. Only this time they had two box trucks full of furniture! There was a bedroom suite for David and me, double bunk beds for the boys, and a bed for Rebecca. They filled up our house with good items they weren't using anymore. We were even given a lounge and a couple of living room chairs.

I was so grateful for all of it, but the items I was *most* thankful for were the practically new washer and dryer that had been sitting in someone's attic! By that point I couldn't hang clothes outside anymore—it was too cold, and they wouldn't dry. David had bought me a portable clothes hoist (a rotary clothesline) that is supposed to go outside, but I would put it over the heating vent so the hot air would dry things. But when it came to drying the sheets, it was not easy. I hadn't known how we were going to survive through fall and winter—and now I had a washer and dryer. It was absolutely wonderful.

With the school at the end of the street where all the families in the neighborhood sent their kids, word got out fast about us and our needs. I had also made quick friends with a woman, Kay Smith, who lived farther down the street, and when she went grocery shopping, she'd buy extra, and on her way home, she would drop them off with a knock on the door. Plus her brother was a hunter, so they also gave us deer meat. Then a neighbor loaned us their car in the evenings to go to the grocery shop or wherever we needed, which was very nice. God's provision came from all directions!

One day Kay arrived to drop off some groceries, and I invited her in to see the "new" furniture. What she saw was a dark-brown corduroy couch and ugly orange, brown, and gold-striped living room chairs. Her mouth dropped open when she heard me say, "Isn't God amazing how the furniture all matches?" This was a different perspective that blew Kay away. But I say the glass always needs to be half full. Otherwise we can miss God's hand in providing for us.

* * *

One "wow" moment for me was when the people who lived across the street came over with a plate of chocolate chip cookies to welcome us, and they asked us what church we went to. I thought this was *hysterical*. In Australia, you might be the only person on your entire street who went to church, so for them to be so bold as to ask right out what church we went to—as if it were a normal thing to ask—took me by surprise. It even seemed to be *expected* that we went to church. Then, to top that off, they actually *invited* us to their church! I mean, it was sort of a jaw-dropping moment. They were so overt about their faith that they would, one, expect us to go to church, then two, invite us to their church . . . As I said, it was a "wow" moment for me.

One of the more special memories I have during this time was being invited over to Greg Nelson's house for dinner. Our family didn't get invited to that many places because we are a *lot* of people. The kids knew we were going to the home of the people who'd arranged for all our furniture, so they were excited, and we all arrived feeling very appreciative.

While we were there, Greg mentioned he was not doing too well—he had been having a lot of back pain. In response, Joel, who was then seven, came up to me and said, "Mum, we need to pray for him."

I turned to David and said, "Joel wants to pray for Greg."

David then announced that Joel wanted to pray for Greg, so both of our families made a big circle and held hands while Joel led us all in prayer for Greg's hurting back.

It was one of those overwhelmingly proud and significant moments for me as a parent. Joel had seen us praying for our real, active needs, and in turn his simple faith came out with Greg. Whenever I see that from any child, I feel encouraged. If I have a single life lesson out of that, it's the importance of sharing our needs with our kids rather than keeping our needs from them. As adults, we so often look at our circumstances with nothing but logic as to why this or that can't happen. Or all we may see is a negative, hard place with no way out. But children don't see things the way we do. They see through eyes of pure and innocent trust. They expect us as their parents to look after them, so when they see us as parents looking to our heavenly Father with trust, they do too. It is why God asks us—requires us—to come to Him like a child. In hard moments, I can see why.

* * *

By October, David had met with a fair number of people, one of them being Wes Yoder, a booking agent who'd had us all over for dinner a few times since we moved there. I was about seven months pregnant when he and his wife invited David and me over again. I had a due date in early January, and up to that point in my pregnancy, I hadn't seen a doctor. Everything seemed normal, but since I knew we were not going to be back in Australia for the delivery, I asked Wes's wife who she would recommend, and she wholeheartedly recommended her own doctor to me. David then called him to tell him of our situation and that we didn't have a lot of money or health insurance, and the doctor said he'd be glad to see me and work with us on the financial part. He also happened to be a lovely Christian man, so it was all quite a relief to have found him.

As it turned out, I was anemic (which was no surprise), plus he said he'd prepare in case I needed to have a hysterectomy after the delivery—possibly even an emergency hysterectomy—because I had had so much bleeding after I had delivered Josh. My previous doctor had said I shouldn't have any more kids because my uterus was worn out. But I had already been praying about this pregnancy and felt God's peace about having one more baby.

I believe God is the giver and the taker of life and that we can take God on our journey, or we can follow His journey for our lives. So I submitted to Him the idea of even having another child after Josh was born, and I was led to a word in 1 Timothy that says, "Women will be saved through childbearing, assuming they continue to live in faith, love, holiness, and modesty" (2:15). In context, I knew this verse was not about my exact circumstances, yet I felt as though God was promising me that I would be okay going through one more childbirth. So

I stood on that promise and considered just how much of a gift it was that Libby was conceived on one of the darkest nights of our lives up to that point. That is why her full name is Elizabeth, because the name means "gift of God."

* * *

About the same time I met my new doctor, fall was approaching, and one day the kids and I didn't have much to do after their schooling lessons. We'd never had the novelty of deciduous trees before, so we borrowed rakes from our neighbor and raked our front yard. Just imagine the sight of a very pregnant woman out in the yard with six kids raking and piling leaves! Our house was located on the main road leading into the neighborhood, and people were driving by and yelling things like, "Hey! You guys are doing a great job! Will you come over and do my yard? I live six houses down!"

So we did. Then someone else would drive by and yell at us, and we'd get another job . . . then another. We got to know the people in the neighborhood just by raking lawns. Plus they paid us quite well, which helped to put food on our table. I also got to know two people that I'm still friends with today—all from raking their lawns in those first few months. The Lord was answering our prayers for provision in multiple ways. He was looking after us, and we were very encouraged by it.

In November, my parents came to stay with the family and me as David and Rebecca were due to fly back to Australia for the wedding of a young woman who had worked for David for about ten years. Rebecca had committed to being a junior bridesmaid. In order to pay for the flights, we'd had to cash in some of our return tickets. Even though it was hard to say goodbye to David and Rebecca, I was very glad to see my parents and for them to join us in our new home. They planned to be with us for Thanksgiving and Christmas—and of course be here for the birth of the baby, who was due at the beginning of January.

In the meantime, the neighbor who had been loaning us their car came over and said they had discovered their insurance wouldn't cover us driving it, so they'd have to drive us, which was a hard moment for me. Having some freedom in the evenings was a pretty big deal, and now that was gone. But with all the ways God was providing, we had to believe something else would open up, and as a family we continued to pray for jobs, for money, and for a car so we could be more self-sufficient. He once again came through.

* * *

It was not long before Thanksgiving, while David and Rebecca were still in Australia, when we got a call from a guy named Jon Mohr inviting us to a homeschooling

Thanksgiving dinner. He had heard about us from Kay Smith, who continued to support and encourage us in very practical ways through those difficult days. I said to him, "I'd like to, but we don't have a car. We haven't got any way of getting there."

He said, "I'll pick you up."

"No, you don't understand," I said. "My parents are here, so there are eight of us. We don't fit into a normal car."

He reassured me it was fine and that he'd work it out. And sure enough, he showed up with a church van, picked us up, and took us to his home for dinner.

Everyone at the dinner was really nice, and after the meal, Jon cornered me and started asking why we were here in the US—he wanted to know what was going on. I answered his questions as honestly as needed, and then he went on to talk to some other people. By then, I was getting tired and could see that the kids were, too, but I didn't want to be rude by interrupting. I finally approached him and asked if he would mind taking us back to our house, please.

He handed me what looked like a set of keys for a Toyota of some kind and said, "You can take yourself."

I looked at the keys. "No, no, no, I can't take these. I've learned from my neighbor that if I were to get in an accident while driving someone else's car, they can get sued and lose everything."

He looked at me and said, "God has told me to let you drive this car. If you have an accident and I get sued, then that's in God's plan. He wants you to have this car."

I was taken aback. His generosity and his faith were a *lot* to take in.

So we drove home in his brand-new Toyota Previa!

* * *

Our first Christmas in America will be one that stands out to me as no less than miraculous. I've always taken birthdays and Christmas fairly seriously, so it was weighing on my mind as to what we were going to do to celebrate. Looking back, it's obvious that God was right there, working in ways we hadn't anticipated.

It all started the first Saturday in December when Jon and his family rocked up and surprised us with a day of celebration at our house. First, they brought us our first *real* Christmas tree to decorate, including the lights and decorations to put on it. It was a very big deal because Australia's Christmas trees are more like the Charlie Brown kind you have here—not very pretty. But the tree they brought was absolutely magnificent. And Jon's wife had cooked meals for dinner, and they all just loved on us. It was such a joyous time.

The Mohrs' surprise was especially meaningful because about this same time, David's employment with the artist he'd come to work for was discontinued. In a meeting, David was told they were sorry, but they just couldn't employ him anymore. So once again, David was without work. Only this time, we were on the other side of the world, and we no longer had enough return tickets. Given this situation and with Christmas approaching, I was preparing the kids in a way by telling them it was going to be different that year. I think I even told them that Santa would have trouble finding us since we had moved so far away from where we were the year before. This was hard for me, but the kids disagreed with me because they thought Santa *always* delivers.

As we got further into the month, I asked David about taking a little money out to at least go to the dollar shop. I knew we couldn't get much, but it was important to me for the kids to have *something* to unwrap. But David said we just couldn't do it—money was pretty scarce.

Not long after that conversation, I got a call from the local school where Greg Nelson's son was in second grade. His teacher had asked the class if they knew of a family they could sponsor, and he'd approached her and said he knew of a family with six kids right down the road. The teacher called us to get an idea of our situation, the ages of the kids, and what they might want. And not long after that, we got a knock on the door, and there were more presents delivered than we'd ever had under the tree before! The kids got so many practical and nice things—it was all quite incredible.

To this day, I tear up when I think about it because it made me realize something about God I hadn't realized before. He says He promises to provide for our needs, but Christmas presents for kids aren't a need, they are a want. Yet, through the kind act of a seven-year-old boy speaking out to his teacher, God not only provided for our needs, He fulfilled our wants. He made us feel so loved and made it clear, once again, that He is always with us and looking after us. He also made it clear never to underestimate what a child can do when they are given the chance.

It was one of the most memorable Christmases, and I will always be humbled and very grateful.

* * *

I can't think of a more wonderful way for our first year in America to end than not only celebrating the birth of Jesus but also the birth of my own child. The baby wasn't due until January, but the doctor said that if I waited until going into labor, I might not necessarily get him for the delivery—he couldn't guarantee which doctor I'd get. Since we had established a relationship, he wanted to be there to help me, and he preferred I book a time to come in so he could induce.

So on December 29, all of the family, including Mum and Dad, piled into the van and excitedly headed to the hospital, and right away they took me upstairs to begin prepping. Meanwhile, David handled the admissions. The woman processing the admission said she couldn't find me on record for having paid the one-thousand-dollar deposit. She said the hospital would not have allowed an uninsured person to book in unless the deposit was paid. Well, no one had ever said anything to him about paying a deposit—it was the first he had heard of it. And the catch of it was that there was nothing she could do at that late stage because they were already prepping me, so they weren't going to kick me out! I see that whole "coincidence" as one more miracle God orchestrated on our behalf so that the delivery would happen as planned with my doctor of choice.

Before we went to the hospital, I had told the older kids that they were welcome to come in and watch the delivery if they so chose. I had not had an ultrasound, as it would have incurred more expense, so at the time we had no idea of the sex of the baby. Mum and Dad planned to stay with the little kids in the waiting room, and at first, I had the older three with me. But as it got closer to the delivery, only Rebecca, who was fourteen then, stayed. Daniel, who was twelve, and Ben, who was ten, started to find it too intense and said, "We're outta here!"

Rebecca had never seen a birth, and I was a little hesitant as to how she would handle it without any preparation, so I kept telling her what would happen next. She was amazed that I could predict what was coming next. Then, when the baby delivered, what a shout of celebration happened when, after five brothers, Rebecca witnessed the birth of her little sister!

Elizabeth Helena Smallbone was born December 29, and her birth was a gift from heaven. It felt to me as though she was a smile from God. I immediately thought of bookends, with a girl being my first child and a girl being the last child, and all boys in between.

Another miracle was that despite all the preparation we did for an emergency hysterectomy, it wasn't needed. There was minimal bleeding, unlike Josh's delivery, and the next day I told the doctor, "I'm really sorry about all the fuss. I don't know what happened, but I'm glad everything worked out so well."

And he said, "Honey, what I gave you would have stuffed up a hose!"

All I knew was things couldn't have gone more smoothly, and David and I felt very blessed to have another girl in our arms. It all felt so right.

CHAPTER SIX

MORE WORK, MORE WAITING, AND *FINALLY* A BREAKTHROUGH

*We can rejoice, too, when we run into problems and
trials, for we know that they help us develop endurance.
And endurance develops strength of character, and
character strengthens our confident hope of salvation.
And this hope will not lead to disappointment.*
Romans 5:3–5

Into the new year of 1992, we continued to see God provide in ways we didn't see coming. First, there was the doctor's bill, as well as the hospital bill. When the doctor's bill came in, it was over double what we would have paid in Australia, even though it was for only two months of care. David called the doctor and asked him if he remembered that he would help us with the bill. He said, "Yes, of course!"

With that, we were expecting him to reduce the bill by about 10 percent or so, but instead, he asked, "What would you normally pay in Australia?"

David said, "About three thousand dollars."

And the doctor said, "That's fine. Just pay that."

We were blown away. But before we could even pay the new amount, we were even *more* shocked when we got a phone call from the doctor's office saying that the bill had been paid in full! To this day we have never found out who paid that bill.

A few months later we got the hospital bill, and David called them up about a payment plan. They asked how much we could afford, and we went back to them with a proposal of two hundred dollars a month, which they accepted. There were a few months that even that amount stretched our budget, and David would have to call them and let them know. David was so impressed with the way they worked with us that when we finally paid it all off a few years later, he called them up to say thank you. I don't think the finance department had ever had that experience before.

* * *

Another blessing God gave us was that David picked up another management job for a very young artist named Eric Champion, so we were able to get by again. But while David brought in two thousand dollars a month, our rent alone was a thousand a month. Between the kids banding together and helping, and the people in the neighborhood donating and providing jobs, we made it work.

Rebecca started babysitting and cleaning houses, but a lot of homes were so big she'd come home exhausted. I said, "Let's just do it together, then we can knock it out in half the time." A couple of places were so big—five to six thousand square feet—I'd take Daniel or Ben to help. They would mop the floors while Bec and I did more of the finesse work. Between babysitting and cleaning, Bec literally helped put food on our table.

We also started going to The People's Church. When we arrived, it was pretty funny how we stood out because there were so many of us. Wherever we went, it was obvious who we were. One couple who used to sit near us found out about our story. The husband worked for Murray, a company that manufactures lawn mowers, and they both knew we didn't have a mower.

Well, when springtime arrived, they rocked up at the house and gave us a brand-new push mower *and* a riding mower—which led to new opportunities. Just like the previous fall with raking, we'd be out cutting our lawn, and people would ask us to do theirs. So that's how we started mowing and landscaping and gardening. All of the jobs were helping us financially, but more than that, I could see that the kids felt very worthwhile and very needed.

* * *

It's amazing what kids can do. Our needs as a family unit caused them to buck up. They learned early on that not everything was about them; it was about the family as a whole. Not to say there weren't times of testing on their part. I still have this mental image of being out working together one day. Libby was one, Josh was about three, and Luke was six. Daniel was using the mower to push leaves into piles while the other boys would hold a tarp, then drag it to where we were depositing them. While this was going on, Josh pushed Libby around in her stroller. Everyone had a job.

Well, at one point when we were all working like crazy, I looked up and saw Luke sitting on the mower with his feet up on the steering wheel. I looked at him and yelled, "Luke! What on *earth* are you doing?"

He looked at me and said, "I gotta rest!"

And I said, "No, you *can't* rest! Get down here and work with the rest of us!"

I was tired, so I knew everyone was tired, but I also knew that when everybody worked together, it helped keep us all going. When you see one person slack off, it can affect the others and give the message that they can slack off, too, and then the task becomes overwhelming to those who are still working.

I also felt that us working together was about more than just the work itself. Each job was an opportunity for everyone to contribute what they could for the good of the whole, and I think the kids knew it deep down. They learned from a young age that they had a job, and every one of them was important. It makes me think of 1 Corinthians 12:18–20, which says, "Our bodies have many parts, and God has put each part just where he wants it. How strange a body would be if it had only one part! Yes, there are many parts, but only one body." And all of those parts are needed for the body to function the way God intended. Even down to little Josh, at three, pushing Libby in the stroller to keep her occupied and amused. Plus, after we'd finish, there was the satisfaction and reward of knowing we'd completed a job well done, and that we did it together.

By this time, Daniel had started working for a friend that I met while raking lawns. He would go with her on Saturday mornings to a flea market and sell T-shirts and hats. He also discovered that he loved the challenge of seeing how far he could stretch a twenty-dollar bill at the grocery shop. Between clipping coupons and meal planning, he did a good job buying as much as he could with what money we had. It was a challenge to him that he enjoyed.

To this day, I am still so touched by the graciousness of all the kids. Whenever they earned money—Rebecca and Daniel being the older and primary ones—there was never, ever a question about whose it was. Each time they'd hold up the money they'd earned, hand it over, and say, "Here's what I got." They didn't ask if they could keep any of it. It was what we all did. It's just the way it was.

I know now that those hard years when the kids helped earn money were formative ones. First, they learned how to work hard with a good attitude. Attitude has always been important to me. I have a statement that I saw lived out with the kids: "Attitude comes before action!" Keep the attitude positive, and the positive actions will follow. Even back when their little hands started putting stamps on envelopes, they were taught not to just whack it on at any angle but to care about the positioning of it. What they did was important, but the way they did it was just as vital.

Second, they gained self-worth because they felt valuable and needed. They knew that no matter what they did, they had a purpose in the greater good of our family.

And third, they learned how to work together and accept each other for where they were in age and ability. They were also able to rise in responsibility as they learned different tasks, which brought fulfillment and satisfaction. These principles held them in full stead later as we toured and came to rely on and depend on one another. We wouldn't have been able to do it otherwise.

* * *

Not long into the year, I began to have a lot of peace that Libby would be our last baby. I had established our family as patients at the local health department's clinic for when any of the kids got sick. To save money, I went to them instead of the obstetrician for my postpartum examination. I got to know the lady there really well, and during my postpartum visit, she brought up contraception and other alternatives. I wasn't keen on David having a vasectomy because I was the one who shouldn't have any more kids. If something happened to me, he should still have the choice of having more kids if he wanted.

So I asked about having a tubal ligation. She said they didn't do them very often and only when one was offered by a doctor, but she put me on a list just in case.

A few weeks later, she called. "Hey, we've just been offered a tubal ligation. Are you still interested?" I said yes.

The decision for the operation was between another lady and me, and apparently there were some definitive guidelines for being eligible. So I eagerly agreed to answer a string of questions, and I was astonished that none of them had to do with US citizenship! It didn't matter that I wasn't yet a citizen of the country, and I qualified just like that.

She let me know the date, time, and location, but for some reason, as it got closer to the day, I confessed to David that the whole setup felt dodgy to me. I felt uneasy. Up till then, I had always had private health and was more in control of caring for my body. I didn't even know who the doctor was. I had always chosen my doctor, but for this, the lady had only given me the time and place. I was just supposed to show up without a clue about the procedure or anything. I felt out of control and vulnerable. David and I prayed about it, and we both sensed that it was still God's way of providing, so I kept moving forward.

When we drove to the address they gave, I remember feeling weird going in. Right away they took me back and started prepping. David wasn't in the room yet, and I didn't want to feel so nervous, but it was hard to shake it off.

The nurse came in and said the doctor would be in shortly to say hello before they took me to the operating room. After she left, I still felt uneasy.

And then in walked the doctor—and it was the same doctor who had delivered Libby! Of *all* the doctors in Nashville it could have been, it was the only one I knew! It turned out that his expertise was not just obstetrics but microsurgery. It was amazing to me—the doctor could have been a *quack*, but no, he was an expert and one that I knew. Once again, the provision of God was unbelievable, and it left me *wowed*. I felt so loved and known by Him. He knew I was out of my comfort zone. He knew I felt vulnerable. And He went above and beyond to care and provide for me once again.

* * *

By fall, the kids and I went back to raking leaves again, but now we had the mower to help us. I wasn't feeling quite as worried as I was the previous year, because we had a little more money and felt more settled. Plus by now we had seen so many different examples of God's provision—so many little miracles. We were still basically living hand to mouth, but even so, we were able to hire an immigration attorney to help us apply for extensions on our visas. And David was still trying to get a contract for Rebecca.

Christmas was once again approaching, and by then a lot more people had heard about us, with word reaching a small Christian record company called Paragon. They ended up sponsoring our second Christmas for the kids. So again, we felt very blessed and cared for.

By the beginning of 1993, David met with Greg Nelson and another record producer named Bill Deaton, who thought they'd gotten a deal for Rebecca with Word Records. They were considering either her or one of two other artists, and they were prepared to pay a ten-thousand-dollar advance, which was a *big* deal for us. We were very excited and hopeful that *finally* a door would open, but as it got closer to the date for deciding, we were told the deal had fallen through at the last minute.

David and I were stunned and thought, *What on earth?* We had been working *so* hard, and to have another door close . . . It is the only morning I can remember when neither of us could get out of bed that day.

Even with that disappointment, God kept encouraging us. We'd get an unexpected check in the mail, or someone would stop by and donate something. We'd always get just enough—enough to know that God was with us and that He had not abandoned us. We just kept moving forward and trusting He would provide the breakthrough we were waiting for. I've learned that oftentimes when we want to give up the most on a dream is when it's right around the corner. Looking back, that was the case for us—we were almost there, we just didn't know it yet. All of our prayer and efforts and waiting were about to start to be fulfilled.

* * *

We realized through these early years that we only survived through the support of the local community and especially the Jon Mohr family. They had not only loaned us their new Previa, but they had encouraged and blessed our first Christmas, and continually offered us their friendship. They helped us financially by having Rebecca babysit and clean, but they also gave us ten thousand dollars in order to buy our own van. This was their response from witnessing our disappointment and discouragement from the Word advance not coming through.

David felt he needed to give Jon something in return, but of course we did not have much to give. The only thing he could think of as some sort of thank you was to offer Jon half of Rebecca's publishing. Up to this time Rebecca had not written a song—maybe some little ditties but no proper songs. Jon was quite a prolific songwriter, having written for Christian artists Sandi Patty and Steve Green. He understood the publishing world.

Jon was touched at the offer but at first declined. After David came back a little more forcefully, he said, "Yes, I will accept your offer. But the only reason I will is that I know if I don't accept it, a record company will take all of it. This allows me the possibility of giving it back to you at some later stage."

I tell you this story because God had a bigger plan for this agreement between two friends. In 1996 Jon and Luanne and their family moved to the Ukraine to become missionaries. Over the ensuing nine years, Rebecca's music publishing financially supported the Mohr family into the six-figure range. This is so amazing. God used Jon's obedience and generosity to us and returned his investment multifold. David and I call it "living in God's economy." Put God first and be obedient to Him, and He will look after you. This lesson not only helped the Mohr family but it also impacted our personal worldview: honor God in all you do.

During these years David continued to receive an income from managing Eric Champion, and he continued to visit different record companies. From the time we first arrived to America, David had visited with basically all the record companies in Nashville. One of them—ForeFront Records—had said Rebecca was too young. A year later, David found out there'd been a change at ForeFront and that they had a new part owner / A&R (artist and reper-toire) director by the name of Eddie DeGarmo. So David went to see them once again regarding the possibility of Rebecca joining their roster. David played Eddie the recording we had done in Australia and told him about the worship movement that was emerging from Australia. I think Eddie was intrigued but still not sure. He said, "What's a sixteen-year-old got to sing about?"

David then told him about some of the miracles we had witnessed over the last couple of years, and Eddie was even more intrigued and wanted to see her perform. Rebecca had been practicing a repertoire of Australian worship songs, plus we had found a couple of churches that had her come and perform at their Wednesday night youth groups. So David arranged for her to do a guest appearance at The People's Church during the evening service. Eddie and his daughter Shannon came to the ser-vice and watched her perform.

Following the performance Eddie arranged for Rebecca to be given a development deal with ForeFront Records. Our breakthrough had *finally* come!

* * *

As soon as Eddie met with David and Rebecca to begin working together, he said he did not want her to use the name Smallbone—he didn't think it would be marketable. He said he wanted a name that represented her Australian international heritage and suggested the name Rebecca St. John. Well, Rebecca was quite offended. She said, "You can't just pull a name from anywhere. It doesn't seem real or honest."

David went back to Eddie and told him how she felt, and he then pointed out that his surname DeGarmo is also a distinctive name, and he'd ended up having some stalker issues during his musical career in DeGarmo and Key. He said he wanted Rebecca to have more anonymity than he did, especially considering that she was a young woman—an argument that was hard to ignore.

We wanted to take his advice, but we also wanted a family name that felt authentic and personal. We called my parents to get their advice on any names, and then we called David's mum to see if she had any ideas. Rebecca explained the situation to her, and in David's mum's very gentle way, she said, "What about James?"

This tugged at our emotions because David's father had just died not long before. In fact, it had been a very hard time for David because it was an unexpected death. His father, Jim, had been diagnosed with colon cancer. He went in for a colostomy, which was successful. However, after a couple of days post-surgery in the hospital, he came down with pneumonia. The doctors tried different antibiotics, but nothing worked. They ended up putting him on a ventilator to give his lungs a rest, but his organs started shutting down, and he died. All of his family was in shock.

And the hard part was that David had been unable to go home to Australia to say goodbye or support his family—we did not have proper visas or enough money. Even today, this has been a continual grief for David. Not saying your final goodbye to someone you love—especially someone as close as your father—is so very hard!

So when David's mum suggested the name James, we thought it was just perfect. We could carry a part of him with us, as well as honor him in Rebecca's stage name. Rebecca felt a "rightness" about it, so Rebecca St. James was birthed.

We never regretted this decision. And Eddie was correct—it placed a relative separation between her stage persona and her real life. It has also provided her with some protection, though during her career she still had to deal with stalkers.

* * *

Up till this development deal with ForeFront Records, Rebecca had not really written a song, so writing for an album was a stretch for her. She partnered with other songwriters and managed to write four of the ten songs on her self-titled first album, *Rebecca St. James*, which released January 24, 1994. It was nice to finish out 1993 with life beginning to take shape and having so many exciting new opportunities for her.

I remember that, even though this was an absolute answer to prayer, I started to feel concern about what the industry might do to Rebecca. Even though she had worked hard up to that point—it's not as if she was a spoiled, darling princess—the stage can be a very deceptive platform for a Christian or for anybody. When on that stage, you're in a world that's all about you. But when you're a servant of God and people are applauding you, it can really mess with your head, and it's hard to maintain a godly perspective.

I went to my friend Kay Smith and said, "She's got such a genuine, sweet, authentic, servant's heart, and I wonder if she needs to keep cleaning or babysitting just to keep her head together."

And she said to me, "No, God's got it. She's well-grounded. She'll keep her head together." Her encouragement was what I needed at just the right time.

So after Rebecca got signed, things really did start to turn around for us. We were no longer in the same desperate condition, and we could see the start of something new being built, and it started to take the edge off. It really hit home the day Daniel came home from working at the flea market, where he'd earned about twenty bucks. When he started to leave the money for us, David looked at him and said, "You can keep the money."

Daniel was *aghast*. "Are you *sure*?"

And David said, "Yes, I'm sure. You can keep the twenty dollars; we don't need it."

Daniel still remembers that day when he could keep the money he had earned. I think it's fascinating to hear some of the stories now of the kids' perspective during those times. Even though they were young, they remember the significant moments on our journey. I think that's what God wants us all to do—to remember His goodness and faithfulness. It's what keeps our hope strong and our faith in Him growing.

PART THREE

TOURING AND FAMILY LIFE

CHAPTER SEVEN

FROM LANDSCAPING
TO TOURING

Those who hope in me will not be disappointed.
Isaiah 49:23 NIV

Finally, it felt as though God had parted the waters. Years of praying and waiting and working and hoping for the breakthrough we wanted for Rebecca and ourselves brought us to a brand-new turning point in life. At long last, we could breathe a bit easier, and David could see something new being built.

Soon, David and Rebecca began to travel to do radio promotions and spot dates. Daniel especially enjoyed the time they were away because, at fourteen, that meant he became the man of the house. He loved cutting coupons and finding the best deals, then feeling the satisfaction of staying on budget when it came time to grocery shop. He really became my right hand and loved caring for me and the rest of the family.

It didn't take long for David to resign from his management job with Eric Champion in order to focus completely on managing Rebecca. Then, in May of 1995, David accompanied her on her first tour as support artist for Bryan Duncan and Bob Carlisle in the Slow Revival Tour. It was so exciting for Bec to travel in a tour bus with a band—it helped her feel even more legit as an artist.

At one point, there were some personnel changes on the tour, so Daniel ended up joining them to help manage the merchandise for all three artists. David thought it made sense to have him help since he had prior experience helping my friend at the farmer's market. Merchandising is very hard work with setting up and managing the tables for one artist, but doing it for all three was a challenge—one he was apparently up for. He was fifteen at the time and rightfully very proud that the money he collected equaled the itemized sales—a continual challenge of merchandising. Fortunately, he made some good buddies on the tour, so if he was still working when stage production was finished, they would help him load out.

* * *

Between songwriting and recording, Rebecca was very busy. I was concerned that she was slipping behind in her schoolwork. At seventeen, she was in tenth grade and had just come home from touring for a couple of weeks. When she started sharing some experiences with me and downloading all that happened, I said to her, "Did you get any schoolwork done?" It was on my mind because she had already taken a year to try to finish grade ten, and she still wasn't done. I couldn't help but be concerned because we still had two more years before finishing high school.

She responded, "Well, you know, it's just so hard. I mean you're out there, you're performing, then you've got signing lines. And if I wasn't doing any of that, I had the pressure of songwriting. It was just really, really hard to find the time and energy to focus on schoolwork."

And as I sat there listening, as mums do, and thinking of all the logical responses for why her schoolwork should be a priority, for the first time, I distinctly heard God in my head say the words, "*Shut up*! I don't want her to do it!" Those were His exact words, and they were loud. I knew it was Him speaking because we didn't usually say *shut up* in our family. Thinking back on it, I'm convinced that He had to practically yell something at me to get my attention, because my mind was whirling with what I would say to Rebecca and how I could say it nicely.

Well, His directive worked, and I kept my mouth shut. Deep down, I knew it would be too much for her. I knew God was right and thought, *Who am I to put pressure on her and demand anything from her at this point?* It was hard because God was telling me to do what is opposite of what the world says to do, and even though we had already been living outside any normal box, this was a whole new step for me. But the more I thought about it, the more I *knew* that what I heard was from Him.

A few days later before Rebecca headed on the road again, I told her what God had said to me and that I didn't think she should do any more schoolwork. God had spoken loudly to me that she needed the freedom to devote herself to her career. I could tell that it was a weight lifted off her shoulders. Being the oldest child, she's very responsible and would have taken it on to the fullest degree if she really had to, but I'm forever grateful for God's leading.

I love that God intervened and spoke directly to her situation and released that pressure from her life. To me, the experience showed me the living, active Word—the rhema, leading and guiding specifically to our situation. I think of Jeremiah 7:23 where God says, "Obey me, and I will be your God, and you will be my people. Do everything as I say, and all will be well!" It is His voice that needs to come through the loudest, His voice that we listen to, His voice that we follow.

* * *

Given the work we'd all done since moving to Nashville, David and I both recognized the strength we had when all of us were together. We felt we didn't want Rebecca and him going off by themselves on tours—it was just too hard for them and for us. After all the landscaping, mowing, raking, and cleaning we had done during the past few years, we had learned to work very well together and believed we could carry the same momentum on tours. I was also still homeschooling, which could be done from anywhere, so that wasn't an issue.

So, once we decided that the whole family would start touring together, we purchased a fifteen-seater van, which was a challenge because we had no credit. The guy who ran Tennessee Car and Van Rentals was a Canadian who understood the challenge of not having a credit history, so he had compassion on us and sold us a secondhand rental van. We used the van to pull a trailer that held basic sound equipment, lights, and merchandise. And as we began touring as a family, transitioning from working in yards to working on tours went pretty well. I don't think there was really any question about who would do what—everybody naturally began looking for their new role.

We brought over a cousin of Rebecca's—Jason Francis—from Australia, who's the same age, and David found a sound guy to show him and Ben how to set up the sound equipment. David also found a lighting guy to show Daniel and Joel how to set up and run the lights. The rest of us helped David however he needed. Age or ability wasn't a factor—everyone had a job, just as before.

* * *

In between touring, Rebecca had to write for another album, so the record label suggested she work with a new young producer in town, Tedd Tjornhom. Now eighteen, she had a better understanding of who she was and had more confidence in songwriting, and with Tedd's encouragement, belief, and partnership, she found a more aggressive rock style that was creative and groundbreaking for contemporary Christian music. This resulted in her *God* album, which was released in 1996. Calling the album *God* was a controversial decision, with the distributor saying it should not be done, but Eddie championed the idea through the system, and it paid off—it went gold, and that meant we'd need to prepare for doing The God Tour.

The *God* album could not be performed using tracks, because the music moved from being more traditional to an aggressive rock feel. So auditions went underway for a band, along with hiring a sound guy, which meant we'd need another vehicle for them to travel in. We reached out to a contact who had a John Deere Coachman dealership, and he helped and organized a huge investment for the purchase of two Class A motorhomes. One was for the family, which David drove, and one was for the band, which they drove.

In the meantime, we continued to grow into each of our roles while on the road. The God Tour was a big step forward for the family as everyone continued to help with all of the work. Daniel had discovered a love of working with moving lights, so at seventeen, he went to Texas to take a class that taught how to program a moving light board as well as basic maintenance. He was also in charge of overseeing the boys and assigned Ben and Joel to help set up the lights and the band gear.

Josh, who was only six by then, had a different job—a speaking part in the song "Carry Me High" when Rebecca performed it onstage. He was a tiny little chap with a baseball cap on. The stage would go black, and Josh would climb up on a riser at the back of the stage where the lights would focus on him. He would stand with a microphone in his hand, and he was supposed to say, "Until you find something worth dying for, you're not really living." It's all he had to say. But Josh had a lisp, so what he actually said was, "Untiw you find somehing worf dying for, you're not wealwy wiving." Then it would black out again and he'd disappear! It was so very precious. It was his first responsibility, and he nailed it every time.

After that, Josh helped with the fans. Back then you had fans that blew smoke across the stage, and he would hold one of the fans to help direct the smoke. Then, by about eight years old, he began running the spotlight under Daniel's supervision. One time we had Rebecca's cousin Matt Smallbone go on the road with us, and his job was to help with the other spotlight. So their first night working together, there was Matt, who was about twenty, and Josh, who was so short, he had to stand on a riser because he couldn't see over the people's heads. Matt and Josh wore headphones so they could hear Daniel tell them when to turn the lights on. When Daniel said, "Spotlights . . . come on *now*," it was their job to hit Rebecca with the light, so she was perfectly centered in the circle.

Well, the time came, and Josh heard Daniel say, "Spotlights . . . one, two, . . . *now*," and he turned his on. But Matt didn't do it quite right, and Josh yelled over to him with his lisp, "Matt! Yow didn't *hit* 'er! You gotta do *bettow* than that!"

So instead of getting yelled at by Daniel, Matt got it from eight-year-old Josh! Even at a young age, he took his job very seriously.

Luke's job was to make the mist or fog. You actually had to have a burner and powder to create the fog so it would fill the room. You didn't see just the color of the lights but the actual light rays—with moving lights, it's all about the rays. Luke would sit back with a fan and have to position it to get the effects in just the right places. He did eventually get a machine to do it, but his introduction to helping with the stage was with the fog machine. Later, he ran a spotlight and ended up staying with lighting under Daniel's supervision. Luke looked up to Daniel a fair amount, so he stayed in that arena for most of his formative years.

Not long after Joel started setting up lights and band gear, he started doing the smoke. By the time he was twelve, we were performing in a lot of traditional churches, and we needed somebody to see a vision for our stage because sometimes we had the stairs and choir lofts to deal with. So Joel was taught stage design by one of David's best friends, Rod Boucher from Australia, who was also a performer and had an understanding of the stage. He went on the road with us, and he helped Joel figure out how to manage a crew, design a stage, and be a stage manager.

Even though Joel was into designing and managing stages, David recognized Joel's performance abilities and thought he could be a good background singer for Rebecca. She had a song that David started prepping him for during sound check. Then came the day that David thought he was actually ready to perform. Well, Bec wasn't super keen on having her little brother, who was seven years younger, do this—Joel, at twelve, looked like a kid. But the day came, and when it was time to go out . . . Joel was *furious*. I don't know why he thought he was rehearsing with Bec other than to perform onstage, but he didn't want any of it, and said, "You *can't* make me do this. You are the *worst* parents in the world. How *dare* you ask me to do this!" I mean, he cried, he was so furious.

I said, "Well, it's a bit like teaching someone to swim. At one point, you've got to jump in and swim or you're never really going to learn. Your dad would not say you can do it if you're not ready. He knows when you're ready, and you're ready *now!*"

So he did it, and while he continued to manage the stage, he has also not been *off* the stage since. Sometimes kids, even adults, have to be pushed when God knows we're ready to do what He wants us to do. We may kick and scream that we're not ready, or sometimes we may sulk, but we just gotta get out there and do it.

This also rang true with Rebecca . . .

* * *

As we all navigated our new roles and new routines, Rebecca continued to rise and grow in her abilities. I am to this day impacted by her honest reliance upon God in prayer. At such a young age, she couldn't do *anything*—neither interviews nor performances—without praying about it first, and she's still that way today. That, to me, is one reason why God has honored her—because of her sincere devotion to Him. I also observed how gently He always led her, and when I think about His relationship with her, I sense His smile. To me as a mum, this has meant a lot—to know His smile on her life.

When she was about nineteen, she was preparing to do an event at a church, and the people there said they wanted her to do an altar call at the end of the performance. Well, she had never done one before, so she was unsure of her ability. She said to us, "I can't do that. I just can't."

David went back to them and said she'd never done an altar call before and implied that he was sure they had somebody else who could do it, and they said okay.

That night, Bec sang her songs, then walked over and stood at the side of the stage while another person walked on to do the altar call. It was awkward and stressful for her to have said no to doing it because she's a pleaser, and then to find herself standing on the side of a stage and watching some other guy do it made her uneasy. As he spoke, she could see that he had lost at least half of the audience, and in that moment, she understood why it was important for her to do it—the other guy wasn't the one who had built a connection with them. She was.

God let her see for herself why He'd led her to that place—to watch someone else do it then realize that she *could* have done it. And to me, it showed the beauty of who God is in His gentle leadership and His understanding. He pushed her to try and step forward, knowing she wouldn't want to do it, and He allowed her to sidestep. But then He gave her the assurance and the words and the knowledge that she could indeed do an altar call.

So from then on, she did them herself, and I felt proud that she constantly rose to new challenges for the sake of God's kingdom and in obedience to Him.

* * *

As Rebecca's career grew, one thing that became apparent by then was that while the boys had one another, there were no other girls on the road who were Rebecca's age for any kind of companionship or camaraderie. There are fourteen years between her and Libby, so there was definitely that void in her life (as well as Libby's, to an extent).

To encourage Rebecca, David and I would bring girls on the road with us, one being a friend she had from Australia. They could only be with us three months at a time, though, so we'd plan their visits around when we were on tour. We also knew a family from Australia whose daughters would come and help with merchandising, and then Rebecca could enjoy their company. So we tried different avenues of having people join us on the road just to be a friend.

Another aspect of the business I noticed during Rebecca's teenage years was the weight she felt about her appearance. That period in life is a very vulnerable one for girls, and the pressure to look a certain way was difficult for her. Rebecca had acne, and one of the record company people approached David and made a comment about her skin. They offered to pay for her to go to a dermatologist, but the negative attention it brought her was hurtful. To add to it, they went to David and said she needed to take her clothes and overall appearance more seriously. There is simply a lot of pressure for female artists that male artists don't get.

I remember one situation when we were on the road for a while when her band was with us. We rocked up late morning for a lunch stop, and as we got off the bus, Rebecca and the band guys lined up to get their food. One of the volunteers helping with the food gave her a good look and said, "Oh, you're Rebecca," and she said, "Yeah."

And the volunteer said, "Oh, you don't look like your photos."

Again, it was just another blow for her. I saw the hurt and frustration on her face—a mum knows when one of her kids gets hurt. Her face read, "I can't even leave the bus without being dressed and made-up."

There was—and I'm sure there still is—an irony about the difference between men and women in a public role. For Rebecca, she had to look a certain made-up way, and if she didn't—if her hair was not styled and she had no makeup on—there was no grace given by others to the fact that she'd just stepped off a bus after being asleep for however long. But when the guys in the band would get off the bus, girls would squeal, "Oh, look, they've got bed hair, and they're in their pajama pants!" There was a whole different standard between her and the guys.

Not only did she find the double standards very hard—she was very conscientious and always wanted to do the right thing—but I found it hard to watch as her mum. It was all a little overwhelming, and I could see that she felt more and more isolated in a lot of ways. Even though we were traveling as a family, the boys had each other, plus they were working for her; Libby was too young to be a friend; the band guys were all guys, and a lot of them were married; and the girls we brought out on the road would at times act passive-aggressive or controlling toward her. David was her manager as well as her father, and even though they made a great team, sometimes she did not feel heard. A lot of times I, as her mum, played the middle ground, but even though we had a good friendship, I was still her mum.

When we returned home from touring, she felt disconnected from a lot of her peers and found it hard to feel accepted. Meeting guys was hard as well because of her status.

From David's and my perspective, we wanted her to be strong and encouraged her as much as we could, but we also knew that the isolation was a burden and a drain she would have to learn to manage and carry on her own. As I have gotten older, I continually go back to the strong interplay between the heart and the head. The heart involves our feelings and emotions whereas the head covers our thinking and logic and our faith. Rebecca, in her head, knew she was God's. She knew she was loved. She knew she did not need to earn His favor, and she always took her faith and her prayer life very seriously. But her heart was lonely and yearned for community and connection. This is where the isolation of the road gets very real and very hard.

CHAPTER EIGHT

LIFE ON THE FARM—
OUR FIRST *REAL*
HOME IN AMERICA

I will end your captivity and restore your fortunes.
Jeremiah 29:14

After Rebecca's signing with ForeFront, there was more going on for us than just learning to tour together: the owner of the house we were renting decided he wanted to sell, so we needed to move out. Honestly, the timing couldn't have been more perfect. We quickly found another place for the short term that worked well, but by then Rebecca had her advance, and David and I had built up some credit, so we decided to go halves on our own place.

We went back to the same Realtor who had helped us before and told her we wanted some small acreage with a house, so she found three places to view. The first two we looked at didn't work at all, but when we got to the third place, which had a farmhouse sitting on nine acres, it felt as though God had gone before us.

As we drove up the drive, Rebecca said excitedly, "Oh, I've always *dreamed* about a driveway with trees over-hanging the road!" Then she said, "Oh, there is a *creek*! I've always wanted a *creek*! I *love* this!"

When we got to the house, it didn't look very big—at least not big enough for our family—so we were trying not to let it disappoint us, but when we walked in, Rebecca said, "Oh, a *fireplace*! I've always wanted a *fireplace*!" And as we went farther in, the house seemed to keep going and going and going. It appeared to check off every need—even some of our wants. It all felt so perfect—we knew it was the right place. It was *home*.

It had been built in 1969, and the farmer who owned it, Mr. Hyde, had not done any upgrades since the seventies. It was all dark brown on the main floor—dark-brown paneling, dark-brown vinyl, dark-brown kitchen cupboards . . . Everything was brown. But we didn't see brown. We saw the fact that it was outdated—which meant we could upgrade it the way we wanted—and that he and his wife had six kids ages eighteen down to four years. At that time Bec was around nineteen and Libby was about five. The setup fit us perfectly. Plus we were the first people to walk through the home who loved it.

To add to what seemed like God paving the way, it turned out that David and I couldn't get a bank loan, but we had enough for a good deposit, and Mr. Hyde said he'd work with us. He was so impressed and taken with our family, he agreed to carry the note for the first year. It was such a God provision for us—we were all absolutely delighted!

It was July when we moved in—so in the heat of summer—and the boys would go out on the property and have a grand time. When they first saw all the bush around, they excitedly went out farther to explore, but it was not long before they came back, eaten up with chiggers and ticks! I think everyone knows what ticks are regardless of where they live, but it seems the South is one of the few places blessed with chiggers. In case you don't know, they are a small red mite you can hardly see. They like to crawl up to soft, tender places and bite—fun stuff that we Australians were totally ignorant of!

Well, the chiggers seemed to love Ben because the following morning his feet were so swollen, he couldn't get his shoes on. His feet were covered in red, puss-filled bites. After that experience, all of the boys learned to be *very* respectful of the bush in the summertime—they either doused themselves with insect repellent or waited until cooler weather before doing too much more exploring.

The bugs also explained why the previous owner, who now lived across the street, wore light-colored blue jeans tucked into his big boots, light-blue long-sleeve cotton shirts, and a big hat. One day when he came over to visit—something he did for the following few years just to check in on us—I said, "Mr. Hyde, it's ninety-something degrees outside! You look so hot!"

And he touted, "Well, this is sort of my own air-conditioning system. When I sweat and my clothes get wet, the breeze cools me off!"

We had a very special "God relationship" with him that lasted for years, and his faith in us by carrying the note that first year once again made us feel so loved and cared for.

* * *

It felt so good to finally have a place to really call "home" in America. The farm has been our family's home ever since—David and I still live in the house to this day. Our best years in Sydney were when we lived on five acres, and it was the sale of that house that helped pay for some of our debt after losing the $250,000. So the farm here in Tennessee felt like God giving back to us what had been taken. But He didn't just replace it, He gave back in abundance. I am reminded of the verses in Joel 2:25–26 that state: "The LORD says, 'I will give you back what you lost to the swarming locusts, the hopping locusts, the stripping locusts, and the cutting locusts. . . . Once again you will have all the food you want, and you will praise the

Lord your God, who does these miracles for you. Never again will my people be disgraced.'" Getting our farm was, indeed, a miracle that has blessed us and continues to bless us in so many ways.

* * *

We didn't waste any time putting down roots by investing in some animals. We hadn't had a family dog in five years, so we started with that. There was already a chicken coop on the property, which Ben wanted to fill, so he researched different breeds of chickens and, before long, thirty specially chosen chicks from a hatchery arrived for him to care for. Libby wanted cats, so we found a couple of barn cats to live in the carport.

Another huge blessing of being on the farm was having the freedom to get outside to discover new loves and develop new skills. David found that driving the tractor and mowing the paddocks was very therapeutic. Daniel and Luke loved maintaining the property by mowing and weed eating. Ben bought a bow and would go bow hunting in the woods on the back hills. Bec simply loved sitting outside in the open and enjoying the sights and sounds. Libby loved the animals, especially a horse that was gifted to her—and who is now in his senior years—and I loved the therapy of looking out over the fields and seeing the constant activity.

While we were able to make many special memories and start new traditions on the farm, I do have a few stories that bring out some of my more inglorious moments as a mum that stand out in my mind even to this day. As with all mums, I'm just grateful for God's grace, as well as my kids'.

* * *

Our family is filled with mostly extroverts with strong personalities, except Ben. He was the first one in the family to be more laid back and introverted. He liked to "hide," so to speak, behind other, more outgoing personalities. I imagine there is one of those in every family. Well, Ben used to hide behind Joel, who's two years younger. Joel was what I called "Ben's gopher." If Ben was thirsty, Joel would get him a drink. Joel had this adoration relationship with him, and from a parent's point of view, I felt Ben used Joel at times, which led to some entertaining circumstances. The one I'm leading to was amusing, but also an embarrassment for me.

We had a family tradition that birthdays were taken very earnestly. We would make what we called "The King Seat" or "The Queen Seat." What we'd do is make a special seat for the birthday person, and when they came out of their room that morning, they would sit in their special seat, and they'd be served a breakfast of their choice. Well, it was Ben's thirteenth birthday—I still embarrassingly laugh at this as Ben retells it to me—and Joel got up at the crack of dawn to make Ben's king seat. He used pillows and sheets and blankets and arranged everything so that his seat was all very fancy. Then he wrote out a menu for Ben that listed all the food we had in the house that Ben might like for breakfast. Joel took it all very seriously.

Well, Ben, being a bit of an actor, flowed into the room acting like, "This is my day. I'm thirteen years old now," and sat in his king seat. He decided he would literally "be the king." He demanded this and demanded that, and Joel raced around, doing his best to make Ben what he wanted.

Then, as Ben retells it, he "lorded it up" over Joel. Joel just wanted to please his brother so it would be the perfect birthday for him, and Ben took it as far as he could.

Finally, Joel became very discouraged and teared up—Ben had complained about something Joel had done. I could see Joel's countenance drop, and I started seeing red and thought, *How can Ben treat his brother like this?* And I marched into the room and spanked Ben. On his birthday.

It wasn't one of my finest moments, and I think Ben retells it just to rub it in my face a little. All I knew was I watched Joel begin the celebration with so much anticipation and slowly break down in discouragement. I'm just glad we can all laugh about it today.

Then there was the time Zach Kelm came to stay with us . . .

The same way I grew up with my parents taking in renters, David and I continued the tradition and had a lot of different people stay, and even live, with us on the farm.

Our back door seemed more like a revolving door. There was even more than one occasion we had an entire family who were friends of ours from Australia stay with us.

Well, one of the first young men to stay with us was Zach. He came from Missouri to help David with management of Rebecca, and he lived with us for five years. While he was with us, he bought his first new car, and one day he went out and noticed one of his front lights was broken. He was pretty upset, understandably.

Libby and Josh had been riding bikes earlier, so I found them and asked if they had bumped into Zach's car. Both of them said no.

The mystery continued for a day or two, and by then, we felt that it had to have been Libby who hit the car with the handle of her bike. I took her up to my bedroom and said she needed to tell the truth—I gave her the whole lecture. In the end, she said, "I suppose I must have done it, but I don't remember."

Since I now had the answer, I went to Zach and told him that Libby had bumped it with the handle of her bike and that she would empty her piggy bank and pay him one hundred dollars, and we would pay the difference to get it fixed.

That night we were sitting at the dinner table, and I was sharing with the family that the mystery had been solved—Libby had confessed to hitting Zach's car with the handle of her bike—when Luke piped up out of the

Young love . . . Visiting David's family in Brisbane, Australia, 1973.

David and me on our wedding day, April 26, 1975. My father thought women shouldn't get married until at least twenty-one, but preferably twenty-five. I was the last of my family to get married. Two brothers married their wives when the girls were nineteen and twenty, so he lost his case. We were married five days after my twentieth birthday. I can be persuasive when I want to be.

Our wedding party in front of my dad's church in Turramurra, outside Sydney, Australia. My dad married us. My mum made my dress, the bridesmaids' dresses, and her own dress. Pretty talented lady! Left to right: David's dad and mum; David's younger brother Brian and sister Cathy; David and me; Wendi Quinn, who was a friend from college; David's brother Ian; and my mum and dad.

David and me departing for our honeymoon. In those days you got changed after the wedding and before you left. My mum cornered David on the way to the car and said, "You better look after my daughter." Perhaps that's why his smile looks a little forced.

Me with our firstborn, Rebecca, when she was a little over one. Spring 1978.

Rebecca was a great older sister. Here she is loving on our second boy, Ben, in February 1982. Rebecca was great at caring for her younger siblings. She would create a bed in a clothes basket and rock Ben to sleep when necessary.

At the beach near Sydney on a colder afternoon. I am holding Joel, who would have been about eighteen months old. December 1985.

David would come to America about once a year to meet with managers, booking agents, and record companies. International flights were half off for kids until the age of twelve, so David brought Rebecca (and later Daniel) to the United States just before she turned twelve. Rebecca had a good relationship with Carman. This picture shows Rebecca and Carman with some of Carman's family in Colorado, June 1989.

Getting ready to leave the hospital in Wahroonga, outside Sydney, after the birth of Josh in October 1989. Left to right: Daniel, Luke in front, me holding Josh, Bec, Joel, and Ben.

Rebecca taking charge of raking the leaves in our front yard, using a borrowed rake. Luke is standing in the background. October 1991.

Outside our first house in Brentwood, Tennessee, in November 1991. The kids made a sign to welcome my mum and dad to America. Left to right: Daniel, Joel, Rebecca, Josh in front, Ben, Mum, and Luke.

Christmas 1991. The Mohrs brought and decorated a tree in our living room. Left to right: David holding Josh, me, Joel in the chair with Luke sitting below him, my dad, Ben, Rebecca, my mum, and Luanne Mohr.

A family photo shoot, January 1992. In order of age, from back to front: Rebecca, Daniel, Ben, Joel, Luke, Josh, and Libby.

Dinner at our first house in Brentwood, 1992. Left to right: Libby in high chair, Ben, Joel, Josh in foreground, me, Luke, and David.

Our first winter experience in America, February 1993. It was also one of the first times the kids had seen snow! We made a snowman for each of us in varying sizes. These are the Daddy and Mummy snowmen. They only lasted a day as the neighboring kids came and bashed them down that night. Left to right: David, me, Ben with Josh in front, Daniel, Joel, Bec holding Libby, and Luke.

Saying goodbye to David's mum and dad at Nashville International Airport after their visit with us in March 1993. This was the last time we ever saw David's dad. He died in August 1993, and we were unable to return to Australia. Left to right: Rebecca, David's dad, David's mum, David, Josh in front, Daniel, Ben, Joel, me holding Libby, and Luke.

Luke and me in spring of 1993. When an advance from a Word Records deal for Rebecca fell over, Jon Mohr gave us $10,000 to encourage us. In order for David to feel comfortable accepting the money, he gave Jon half of Rebecca's publishing, even though she had never written a song. We sent money home to Australia for business debts and used some of it to buy this van so we could return the Previa to Jon. The van came with a 13-inch TV/video combo. It was our only TV for many years.

Backstage with Rebecca, 1994. She had just released her first album. At the top of the photo, you can see Rebecca's worn-off signature. Left to right: Rebecca, Daniel, me holding Josh, and David holding Libby.

Joel taking it all very seriously at the lighting console, 1996.

This family photo was taken on the last night of back-to-back tours in the late 1990s. We were all exhausted. Back row, left to right: Ben, Joel, Rebecca, Luke, and Daniel. Front row, left to right: Josh, David, Libby, and me.

Joel when he started doing background vocals with Rebecca in 1997.

At the airport on a European tour in 1997. As you can see, we all look weary. We would travel internationally as a family for the experience and understanding that it gives. Here we are traveling with the band. (Not sure the band always appreciated having us with them.) Left to right: me with Libby, European promoter, Joel in front, Jerry Mowery, Tracy Ferrie, Luke, Daniel, Brad Duncan, Josh in front, Rebecca, David, and Charles Garrett.

Our first family photo at the farm, taken by a friend in fall 1997. Left to right: Libby, Rebecca, Ben at the back, Luke, Josh in front, David, Joel, me, and Daniel.

Rebecca working with her producer, Tedd Tjornhom, on the *Pray* album, which was released in 1998.

Luke was often the favored one to climb the truss and position the lights or change out the chords. On tour, 1998.

Ben taking a photo of himself in a dressing room mirror.

Rebecca performing at EO in the Netherlands, 2000.

Some lovin' on the couch, Christmas 2000. Luke and Joel are on the couch with David and me. Once the kids started earning some money, our Christmases became quite decadent. Sometimes it would take about three sittings to get through the pile of presents.

In Oregon on a day off, traveling and spending time together as a family. We had just walked up to Multnomah Falls. David is doing what he does very well—talking on the phone—but is struggling to find signal. Rebecca is exasperated. Josh is getting out some of his energy by throwing the football. This photo is very real to our life in the early 2000s. It makes me laugh.

The background dancers, Joel and Daniel, rocking out to one of Rebecca's songs in 2002.

Rebecca is finally married. The ecstatic look of triumph after being announced Mr. and Mrs. Jacob Fink, April 2011.

Our family's Christmas Day 2020. We are quite the tribe!

blue, and said, "Are you talking about the broken light on Zach's car?"

I said yes, and he replied, "Oh, I did that!"

My eyes widened and my mouth dropped open. "*What?*"

He answered, "Yes, I hit it and forgot to tell you."

I looked at him, amazed. "Luke, *where* have you *been* the last couple of days?"

Poor Libby. She just sat there and said, "I didn't think I had hit it."

As I said, as hard as any mum tries to raise her kids right, she is still vulnerable to making mistakes, and I'm just grateful for forgiveness and grace to cover the wrongs. Also, there's always the temptation to watch other mums and start to compare yourself and your shortcomings to what appears to be much better parenting skills and having things all together. But it's important to remember that no one does it *all* right. Every mum has her stories and weaknesses that, hopefully, cause her to walk in God's grace one day at a time.

* * *

As the kids grew older, life on the farm didn't slow down. With us touring and traveling so much, the kids felt a little disconnected from their peers. The girls struggled, but the boy who struggled the most was the youngest—Josh. He has always seemed an old soul, even as a young child; he lived in an adult world with a lot of adult responsibilities.

So when he looked at his peers, they terrified him. They seemed immature and untrustworthy.

When we were home, we wanted the kids to be involved in normal activities as much as possible, which included church and youth group. When Josh was in his early teens, I decided it would be good for him to go to our church's youth camp. He had never been before, and he was not very keen on the idea.

I did the pep talk during the drive to church, but when we arrived and he saw all the kids with their bags and pillows, the reality of leaving hit him, and he started crying. I tried to console him, but as much as I did not like to give in, I realized it was too overwhelming for him. I went to tell the youth leader, Darren Whitehead, who was also from Australia. We'd helped Darren get a visa to the US, plus he had lived with us in our basement. I explained the situation—which he understood, knowing the different dynamics of our family—and I'll always look back and smile at how something very special came out of that incident: since Josh struggled with his peers at church and camp, Joel stepped up and invited some of them to the farm, which brought on some fun antics.

Joel, who was in his late teens and still living at the farm, decided to set up a Bible study for the boys from church who were in Josh's age group. The boys *loved* Joel, and the arrangement gave relief to Josh. About once a month they would come over to spend Saturday night at the farm, and Joel would organize paintball wars before dark, which everybody loved, including our own boys. Then, in the evening they would start a bonfire, and as it got later, they'd camp out in the basement, and Joel would lead them in a Bible study.

Ben, ever the storyteller, would take advantage of having a captive audience while they were all outside. He loved telling the boys stories about the farm—although I should probably say they were more like horror stories. Ben's favorite made-up character was a ghost who apparently lived up in our big barn. That particular character still lives on in his imagination, with the stories now being relayed to our grandchildren.

One time Joel told the boys they were going to roast marshmallows over a campfire up in the bush. This was *after* Ben had told them the ghost story. As all the boys sat around the bonfire, Ben, who was accompanied by Libby, went up into the surrounding bush to make loud noises. Meanwhile, Joel interpreted the noises according to the legend of the ghost that the boys had been told earlier. For city kids, it was all pretty scary, and Joel and Ben knew they had gone too far when one of the boys peed his pants!

These are just a few stories that allow me to say, wholeheartedly, that life on the farm has been a blessing beyond measure. They remind me of when I once heard someone say that if you want to survive touring and the music business or maybe even the stage, you need to buy some property. Our family has found this to be true. Our farm has been not only our home but a safe place to return to where we could all stop performing, let our hair down, be in God's creation, and have some fun.

Actually, no matter what you do, this is important for having any balance in life.

CHAPTER NINE

REBECCA'S CONTINUED RISE AND A FEW GROWING PAINS

Don't let anyone think less of you because you are young.
Be an example to all believers in what you say, in the
way you live, in your love, your faith, and your purity.
1 Timothy 4:12

I view America as the land of plenty in many ways—possessions, materialism, and living the high life. It's also the land of plenty regarding spiritual resources. Sometimes I have felt as though Americans are so well-fed spiritually—there is such an abundance of Bibles, churches, and the exploration and freedom of religion (no matter what you believe)—that Christians and people in general tend to exist more in a lukewarm state.

I have felt this way since moving here to America, but it became even more apparent when the True Love Waits movement back in the nineties became pretty big. The organization wanted Rebecca to be the special artist to perform at their conferences, which she was very happy to do. Rebecca has always appealed to young girls, and I feel her authentic heart for God has helped girls to understand their value in Christ. And her message was *far* from lukewarm. She encouraged them to take care in the way they dressed and remain pure until they were married. This was her own personal conviction.

It is very biblical to remain pure, not only in regard to marriage, but in all aspects of our faith. This is explained in 1 Corinthians 6:19–20, which says, "Don't you realize that your body is the temple of the Holy Spirit, who lives in you and was given to you by God? You do not belong to yourself, for God bought you with a high price. So you must honor God with your body." Rebecca's participation in the purity movement ignited a personal passion for the purity message that she has carried throughout her career. It also led to her performing in larger, more commercial venues, which ended up bringing a new hurdle we hadn't anticipated.

* * *

In bigger venues, there are union rules, one being that a kid under eighteen years old was not allowed on the stage, particularly when setting up. Well, one day we showed up at a venue along with our sound guy, Ralph Rivera, who had been with us for a long time. He, along with some union guys who were there, unloaded all the equipment onto the stage. Then Joel, who was around fourteen or fifteen, got on the stage to manage the setup, and that's when the problem began.

One of the union guys didn't miss a beat and said, "Hey, he can't be on the stage. You've got to be over eighteen to be here."

Ralph, who was obviously an adult, piped up and said, "He's the stage manager."

The union guy said, "He can't boss us around. He's not part of the union, and he's under eighteen. He can't tell us what to do."

Ralph said, "Trust me, this 'kid' knows what he's doing, and the concert will not go on tonight unless he is allowed to do what he needs to do."

So Joel entered into an environment where he was working with people with suspicion and a little bit of an angst toward him. Fortunately, he had learned how to grow relationships with others well.

While they were all working and setting everything up, there was a problem with some of the equipment that the union guys had been trying to figure out but couldn't. They eventually gave up trying, but in Joel's mind, you didn't give up. You had to keep at it. He said, "It *has* to be one of the wires. It has to be in the communication."

But a union guy said, "We've changed everything out, and it still doesn't work."

Well, Joel kept working on it until he found the problem and corrected it. By the end of the night, the guys who did not want him on the stage had given him a union shirt. Joel had proved he knew what he was doing.

When I think of all that the kids were accomplishing in such a short period of years, I can't help but think of the verse in 1 Timothy 4:12 that says, "Don't let anyone think less of you because you are young. Be an example to all believers in what you say, in the way you live, in your love, your faith, and your purity." I believe that's exactly what they did—set an example, not only in front of an arena full of adoring fans, but also for the other men who worked behind the scenes during each setup and tear down. But in order for that to have happened, they had to be given work that made them know they mattered.

I think that in this day and age a lot of kids, particularly teenagers, don't feel they matter. Instead of making contributions to their families, they're being completely provided for, which I think robs them of feeling any sense of purpose. That is one thing I don't doubt our kids had: purpose.

* * *

By 1996, Rebecca had released the *God* album, which quickly opened doors for her internationally. Once she locked in on her pop/alternative style—with the help of Tedd Tjornhom—and wrote challenging, God-focused lyrics, she got the attention of the Christian kids in Europe, as well as a big evangelistic conference in the Netherlands called EO (Evangelical Organization). It was a mega conference where fifteen to twenty thousand kids from all over Europe attended and Christian music artists performed over a weekend. They invited Rebecca, and she was very well received.

We then had the confidence to plan her first European tour the following year. We were excited about this because, while American Christian radio played Rebecca, her music did not really fit their sound like it did in Europe. The industry and fans embraced her so much more there—I think partly because she was a bit rocky, and they liked the edge she had to her music. But part of what they liked was that she was overtly strong about her faith and about purity, which was a contradiction to their culture and society, even in the church.

I was actually shocked at how well she was received there—to the point that, at the height of her career, she was actually treated a bit like a pop star with the screaming and yelling fans. I realized then that her strength and overtness were taken for granted here in America—the land of plenty. People, as a general rule, are hungry to be fed by people who are passionate about and sure of what they believe and have purpose in, especially when they don't have such tremendous access to so many resources. Rebecca had both of those qualities—they were a rarity in their culture—so the fans in Europe received her incredibly warmly.

* * *

The trips we took to Europe were special to us not only because of Rebecca's rise but also because we viewed them as wonderful opportunities for us to learn different cultures and see some historical places that would very richly enhance the kids' education. We began to travel quite extensively together there, building some pretty grand experiences. It's also when David got the idea to videotape Rebecca behind the scenes at concerts, as well as our travels as a family. He decided to buy a video camera and give it to Ben, who was about sixteen, to do the videos and document what we did.

Ben had been working under Daniel running the lights for a while. Daniel had learned to program the lights, and Ben would run the program while Daniel then went onstage to do background singing. But that arrangement didn't leave room for Ben to use his own creativity— he didn't have the freedom to use his imagination and do what he thought would look good. Looking back, I wish I'd had Ben's back more by helping to give him the room he needed to express his own talents—I didn't do enough to protect his desires and abilities. Instead, he was always a bit subservient to Daniel, and with Ben's quiet personality, he didn't complain about it.

Well, God had His own way of addressing the situation through the new video camera. We know now that this new role was an inspired assignment from God—it was the beginning of Ben's love of videography. The new job gave him more responsibility that he enjoyed, and the videos spurred excitement from seeing actual visuals to replay from concerts. Videos weren't a thing at concerts then, so seeing his efforts on film brought the performances to life in a whole new way.

When we'd get home from touring, the camera didn't lay idle. Ben and Joel, along with some friends and their younger brothers, would take our old truck up onto the hills to reenact army movie battles. Some were the good guys and others played the bad guys. Ben developed a bloodcurdling scream, and Joel loved the drama of fighting in the woods.

On one occasion Joel had a backpack with a hunting knife in it that he used as a pretend weapon in some of the scenes. He really got into the rough-and-tumble. At the end of the day, on returning to the house, he took off the backpack, and there was blood soaking his shirt. During the tumbling, the knife had cut through the backpack and into Joel's back. He said, "I could feel something, but I thought it was an ant bite."

Off to the ER we went to get stitches—only to find that they had to make a police report because Joel was a minor, and a knife was the weapon. Sons will be sons!

* * *

Ben and Joel not only used the camera to create movies and short films, but they'd also create fun opening videos for the youth group at our church. They created a "Men in Black meets NSYNC" theme called Fugents, and they wrote skits and would act them out as an introduction leading into each youth night's gathering. They'd wear black suits and sunglasses and do choreographed dances together and had a *ball* pulling in some of their friends and making those videos.

I was glad the boys were able to have so much fun in being creative as well as contribute to the youth group, but over time, more and more often they'd ask to go out socially with their friends. It was always the same story: *Everyone* is going. *All* the other parents are letting their kids do this or that . . . I felt that both Ben and Joel were becoming a bit too influenced by American culture, and it concerned me. I picked up on a subtle change in their attitude. I am a big believer that attitude comes before action. Bad attitudes from kids show there are deeper issues going on that need to be looked at more closely.

Becoming an observer of your child and praying for God to reveal to you the child's heart is so very important.

If a child has a disrespectful attitude toward you that is not studied and dealt with, rebellious actions invariably follow. It is why Paul wrote in Ephesians 6:1–3, "Children, obey your parents because you belong to the Lord, for this is the right thing to do. 'Honor your father and mother.' This is the first commandment with a promise: If you honor your father and mother, 'things will go well for you, and you will have a long life on the earth.'"

We love our children and have always wanted the best for them. Honoring us as mum or dad is for their best, as this comes with a promise: that things will go well for them and they will have a long life. If we follow God's plan, then our children will have this promise fulfilled in their lives!

Here in this passage from Ephesians, it also tells us that children need to obey their parents. We, as parents, are told to teach our children to obey. This is at the core of good parenting. If we don't teach our kids how to obey and respect us, whom they can see, how can they obey and respect their heavenly Father whom they cannot see? This was at the core of my concerns for the boys. I was concerned I was seeing them act as if they knew it all and that we were losing our influence and our voice as their parents.

At one point, Ben broke up with a girlfriend, and Joel began to like a girl who was over two years older than him. I remember saying to Joel, "You will have a relationship with that girl over my dead body." Pretty stupid statement, really!

In addition, both boys were starting to care too much about how they looked and appearing "cool." I finally had enough. I thought they both needed a good infusion of Australian culture.

* * *

Just after Ben turned eighteen and when Joel was sixteen, David and I sent both of them back to Australia to the outback for six weeks. One of David's friends named John Phelps owned a cattle property of about twenty-five thousand acres that was forty minutes from the nearest small town. I felt that spending time there working the farm would be a great dose of reality for them to see how others lived. I loved the fact, too, that there was very minimal contact with the rest of the world—they only had dial-up internet that worked only some of the time!

It turned out that farm life in the outback was quite an awakening.

Once they arrived, the boys were put right to work. In the morning, John would drop them off in the middle of the paddocks to pull up fencing—I mean miles of it—and not pick them up until hours later.

They were expected to use machinery on the farm, including a couple of different modes of transport. There was a truck and also a motorbike. Both of these were geared. The boys understood that a car can be automatic or geared, and even though they were not great at changing gears, they knew the principle. However, they had never driven a motorcycle before and did not know they had to change gears or how to. The farmer, John, did not think it necessary to explain such a simple thing to them, as kids on farms know how to drive trucks and motorbikes from about eight years of age.

This colliding of two worlds caused the boys to burn out the gears on the motorbike. John was aghast! He was even more upset when the boys, while using the chainsaw out working on the fence, left it on the ground, reversed the truck, and ran over it! Now two pieces of equipment ruined by these ignorant city kids! He'd definitely signed up for more than he bargained for.

The same went for the boys. Australians have only recently included air conditioners as necessities in their houses. However, twenty years ago they were not a reality, especially in the outback. Sleeping at night was not always a pleasant experience, especially in summer. One night the household was awoken to a loud bang. John got up to investigate the noises emanating from the boys' room on the side porch to find Ben standing dazed in the doorway. He had overheated, which caused a nightmare. He thought he saw something and had sleepwalked and put his fist through the wall, knocking down a picture. I think this freaked everyone out!

Not only did the boys make quite the impression on the farmer's family, but John also made quite the impression on them as well. One day when John was using the tractor to push over a fence post, Joel was helping and somehow got a finger caught between the tractor blade and the post. Joel showed John the damage, and he pulled out his handkerchief and said, "Wrap it up. It will stop the bleeding."

Joel said, "Shouldn't we get it checked by a doctor?"

And John said, "No, it's not that bad. We will doctor it when we get back to the house at lunchtime!"

Joel just stood there speechless.

Even going to church was quite the culture shock. In America, we have attended a large church all the time we've been here, but churches are not big in Australia. So, Ben and Joel were quite the sight dressed in their fancy American clothes and speaking with their American accents.

But the attention they got wasn't enough for them to want to stay. After only a couple of weeks, they had both had enough—they *begged* us to let them leave early and join us on holiday at the beach!

Ben's report from his visit was: "I can't believe that is the country I was born in!"

But I must say, the time they spent there did, indeed, open their eyes to being too sucked into the culture here in America. In fact, with that realization, and with his love of videography, Ben came to David and me and said he wanted to get off the road—he needed to find his own place in his own world. He was also tired of only being known as Rebecca St. James's brother.

So he went out on his own and started his own company called Radiate Films. He started doing jobs for more youth groups, creating moving and still backgrounds to put behind worship song lyrics. He would do countdowns and sell them to churches. And he also moved into video editing. He was the first to leave our family touring, but we were very happy for him as he definitely found his own niche. There comes a time when a parent must cut the cord, and it was his time.

CHAPTER TEN

HOMAGE TO
HOMESCHOOLING

"My thoughts are nothing like your thoughts," says the LORD.
"And my ways are far beyond anything you could imagine.
For just as the heavens are higher than the earth,
so my ways are higher than your ways
and my thoughts higher than your thoughts."
Isaiah 55:8–9

While I'm thinking back and writing about major events in my life, it wouldn't feel complete not to touch on the topic of homeschooling, especially since it's been such a large part of my life and raising the kids. I began homeschooling clear back in Australia when we thought we might move to the US. Some of our best friends, Rod and Vivienne Boucher—who had seven daughters—had taken their children out of public school, and Rod remarked he had noticed big changes in the family. Homeschooling was a whole new concept for me, and his family was the only one I knew who had ever tried it. I was intrigued.

The Australian school year starts at the end of January, and when we were first expecting to go to the States, we thought we'd make the trip in April. With that, it made the most sense not to enroll our kids in the private Christian school they had been attending—they would only be there for a few months. Plus the school had a waiting list, which meant some other poor kid would have to start a few months late after the vacancy became available. Homeschooling would also save us money, which was very tight.

I went to David and explained my logic. He said, "Having all the kids home all day every day will drive you crazy!"

I countered, "It's only for a few months, and since you think that is the case, it will be good for me to find out now whether or not I can handle it. Also it will save us money on the school fees." And that convinced him.

Then, after we got to the US and went through all the zigzags and detours of getting here and trying to settle into a new home, plus the enormous cultural change facing us, it made sense, once again, to keep us together and homeschool at least for the first year. I didn't know then that it would become a permanent path God would set for me that is more outside the box than the way most "normal" families do school. Remember, while home-schooling is a more accepted way to educate children now, thirty years ago it wasn't.

So now, given all the years of experience behind me, I want to speak loudly to other families out there who may listen. I believe that we (meaning general society) to a fault have expectations that traditions such as how we do school must look a certain way. I think that's a detriment. It's also my opinion—and I say this respectfully—that parents baby their kids too much today in the Western world. Too many kids haven't got responsibilities, which robs them of the satisfaction of accomplishing and contributing to a bigger picture. The mindset of so many kids—and even their parents and teachers—is that every day or event is about having fun. There's certainly nothing wrong with having fun, but making that the focus of everything we do isn't real life, especially the Christian life. It's about a whole stack more than just fun.

God entrusts our children to us, and I believe it is our responsibility as their parents to teach them about God and the world He created. I love the verses in Deuteronomy 6:4–9 that say:

> Listen, O Israel! The LORD is our God, the LORD alone. And you must love the LORD your God with all your heart, all your soul, and all your strength. And you must commit yourselves wholeheartedly

to these commands that I am giving you today. Repeat them again and again to your children. Talk about them when you are at home and when you are on the road, when you are going to bed and when you are getting up. Tie them to your hands and wear them on your forehead as reminders. Write them on the doorposts of your house and on your gates.

As parents, we need to bring our faith into the home and practice biblical principles with our children. That means practicing confession and forgiveness, remembering the Golden Rule, displaying the fruit of the Spirit, and knowing who God is and recognizing His hand on our lives.

I can boldly say that I have witnessed the faithfulness of God in fulfilling the following promise in our children's lives: "Direct your children onto the right path, and when they are older, they will not leave it" (Proverbs 22:6). God created each of us for a purpose and gave us unique gifts and abilities. Teaching our children about their calling and helping them understand their vocation is one of our responsibilities as their parents. The sense of purpose that God has a special plan for their lives transforms our children from thinking that life is all about them to realizing they have a particular task and mission in life.

Our kids obviously didn't grow up sitting at home or in a classroom all day working from books. They grew up in an adult environment that was very stimulating for their minds. They were taught how to learn. They obviously had a desire to do so, which I think is the major focus of homeschooling.

When you give kids the skills and the desire to learn, they'll learn. If you provide them with the right environment, they'll learn. So if they don't complete the required learning in the traditional and "normal" sense, as long as they possess the brain maturity to understand concepts, they will learn.

This being said, one of the greater challenges a homeschool mum faces is how to create a school at home that looks different from regular school and how to implement lessons into all the activities of daily life. For me, the challenge I faced was working around all the touring.

* * *

By the fall of 2000, Rebecca's fourth album titled *Transform* had released, and we were all gearing up for the Transform Tour the following year. We were scheduled to hit the road for over thirteen months with what felt like back-to-back-to-back performances or tours. As we got closer to the start date, I remember thinking, *Oh, my goodness gracious! What's my expectation of school this year?*

The tour routine by then was that the kids would rock up and start loading in at eleven in the morning and work until twelve o'clock at night. They had a volunteer crew, but they had to manage the crew as well as work alongside them to set up, tear down, and pack up the truck. With a schedule like that, it was hard to even think about schoolwork and teaching or marking papers. I just wanted there to be time for everyone to be "off" when they weren't working, but I also knew the tour was going to pretty much cover the gamut of the full school year, and I didn't know how we'd do it.

I was very conscientious of the realities ahead. As their mum, I loved my kids, and I wanted to do my best for them. My fear was that, as their teacher, they were going to get to the end of their schooling and say, "Mum, what did you *do*? What did you *do* to us? What if God calls us to work somewhere and we don't have the skills to do it? We're gonna have to go back and study just to get up to scratch! You messed us up big-time . . ."

That was my fear, and I think it's a fear for a lot of homeschooling mums—that they're not teaching their kids right, that their kids aren't learning in a timely manner. They wonder if their kids are learning all they need to grow and succeed. I also think one of the biggest pressures or challenges is not burning out, given all the responsibilities and hats a mum wears in making sure their kids are keeping up with their peers, academically or otherwise. I was more than a little concerned about the year ahead.

As I looked at the touring schedule, I prayed, "God, what am I going to do? What do I even plan for this year's schoolwork and assignments?" I called to Him and sought Him hard, needing very specific answers for how I was to view the situation, what I was to do, and what I should plan. And then, for a second time, I specifically heard God speak directly to me (and I'm glad to say it wasn't as rough as the first time!). He said, "*I'll* teach them what they need to know." The words were very clear, and they gave me the exact confidence and peace I needed. I believed what He said and was ready to go forward, taking His lead and trusting that He knew best.

When we went on the road, we read a lot of historical fiction and biographies about major historical figures, events, and different ancient cultures in Europe and America. We also focused a lot of reading on science. Then, when we were home for a few weeks at a time and were able to take some downtime and get replenished, we'd do as much of the bookwork as we could before hitting the road again.

I remember there being times when the kids struggled to wrap their heads around certain algebra or geometry concepts. They'd ask, "Why do we have to learn this? When am I going to use this?" Their minds and lives were so practical, they thought some of it was ridiculous. I explained that there are certain things in life we need to learn for, if nothing else, the thought process it takes to find an answer. Oftentimes, when they struggled, we'd put the work down, go on the road for three weeks, come back, sit down in the same place, and all of a sudden the light would come on, and they'd get it. This amazed me!

What I find incredible now that I'm on the other side of their lives (they're all adults and have their own careers) is that our kids learned on a day-by-day basis a whole array of life skills our school systems do not teach kids today. They learned self-responsibility. They learned they had a purpose and that they were needed. They were inspired to achieve, and they were given the opportunities needed to keep growing into higher achievements. They learned that when you don't know how to do something, you don't give up—you keep trying until you figure it out, or you find someone else who knows and learn from them. They learned to watch and observe and understand. They learned the social skills of how to look at people in the eye, introduce themselves, and show interest in others. They honed skills while continually working with adults, and I believe they rose to a higher level than most because that was the expectation David and I set for them. In the end, they didn't grow and learn solely out of a book. God indeed taught them what they needed to know and gave understanding as they were ready—not just in their schooling but through the work they had to do.

The boys didn't just do their own jobs as individuals— they helped their siblings learn what they knew, and they worked alongside one another. They learned how to put the pieces of a stage together in the order needed for everything to be just right. They learned what chords went with what, how to create new sounds, and how to affect the mood of a room with lights and fog. The work they did took a lot of general logic and development, it took creative thinking skills they would never have gotten from a book, and it took a lot of spiritual awareness to write the songs and connect with an audience in a way that pointed to God. I didn't think about all of this then, but looking back, I've realized that working hard, completing tasks and receiving satisfaction from a job well done, working with adults, being able to effectively communicate with adults and one another—they are all huge life skills.

I can think of one guy who traveled with us and helped us on the road who could set up everything himself. He worked like a Trojan. But he did all the work by himself. He could not or would not delegate or explain the setup process, so the volunteers didn't work with him. And yet our sons grew up in an environment where they not only learned how to do the jobs but learned how to communicate, delegate, and make sure everything was done properly. They did this with the show volunteers, stage crew, and with one another. They even grew to anticipate a problem and act on it before it ever became a problem. All of these aspects are so important. They became quite the team.

Kids can learn a great deal by observing more experienced people doing something. Josh proved this one night on the fly during a concert. I'll never forget it . . .

* * *

Josh had turned thirteen, and by then Luke was in his junior year of school and in charge of running the lights. Daniel had actually left the road for a period of time to run some of his own business opportunities, so he would program the lights ahead of the tour, and Luke would run them.

One night, we were preparing for a concert out in the middle of Kentucky. Luke was back in Nashville, playing in a basketball tournament with a local Christian school, and afterward, he was to be driven by his cousin, Mike Smallbone, to the concert. They were to arrive before it started but would not be there in time to set up. As the hour for the concert approached, we knew Luke was supposed to be on his way, but this was before good coverage for cell phones, so we couldn't communicate with him to find out exactly what time he would arrive.

So Josh, at thirteen, walked up to David before the concert and said, "I can run the lights."

David looked at him. "Oh, you're *sure* you can run them?"

And Josh said, "Yeah! I've watched how Daniel and Luke do it. I know how to run the lights. I don't know how to do all the positions, but it should be fine to use the ones from last night. I know how to run the lights."

Well, normally, Rebecca would do the opening, then there would be a support act that came on, and then Rebecca would close. But since we were afraid Luke would be late, David decided to put the support act at the beginning to give Luke more time to arrive. So the support act went on, then we had a bit of an intermission, and I noticed Josh kept looking at the door. I could tell he was waiting for Luke to get there.

I said to him, "Josh, do you *really* know how to run the lights, or is this all bravado?"

And he said, "Yes, well, I know how to run the *first song*." And I knew immediately that it was going to be interesting if Luke didn't show up in time! I mean, Josh still couldn't even see over peoples' heads—he was too short. He had to stand on a box so he could see over the crowd.

The first song is *so* important to get right, but it was time to begin. So on went the show, and . . . Josh got all the lights right on beat! He did it! It turned out that Luke didn't show up until the last song, and Josh ran the lights for the whole concert.

I said to him afterward, "How did you know how to do that? You've never done it before!"

And he said with a smile, "Well, I just watched the boys do it."

That is something significant for Josh, and I've seen it grow him in different ways since: he learns by observation. And many other kids can do this as well. Being in an environment that inspires and stretches the mind is such an effective way for kids to learn more than we often give them credit for. And there are no books involved.

Another example for learning makes me think of when Josh was fourteen and we were doing arenas with the Newsboys. By then, Josh was in charge of merchandising. The Newsboys' merchandising guy was very good—he had his own company and was one of the best merchandisers out there.

When you're doing stadium or arena tours, you could be settling with the venue at midnight. So there Josh was at fourteen with the responsibility of not only balancing the actual income to what was sold, but then working out percentages to pay the venue. It's a lot of responsibility for an adult, let alone a kid. But Josh excelled at it, and it was a great opportunity to learn not only life skills but math skills.

On this particular tour, Josh had this determination that, for one night, he was gonna get the best position for merchandise in the arena. The guy with the Newsboys, who was about forty years old, always got the best position, and Josh would be left with the number two spot, which didn't make as much in sales because of the location. The bands were billed as coheadliners, so for Rebecca to always get the second position wasn't entirely fair. Josh was determined to get the best position and sell more merchandise than the other guy did.

One day, we happened to get to the venue first, so Josh got the prime position. He'd started setting up his merchandise when the other guy rocked up and said, "Oh, no, this is my position. You're gonna have to move. We're gonna move you over here."

But the guy's wife, who was working with him, stopped him. "No, he is not moving anywhere," she said. "You're going to let him have that position."

I believe she did that because Josh had built relationships with her and all the people doing merchandise (that dude actually took Josh under his wing most of the time). In any case, Josh kept his position, and that night he beat the Newsboys for the amount of merchandise sold. Between being on point with all the math, having good personal relationship skills, and knowing when to seize an opportunity, he was able to experience a very significant wealth of satisfaction for a job well done!

* * *

I never had any ambition to be a teacher. I never had any desire to homeschool. But I am a big believer in following God's leadership. It was His idea for me to go this route in life. And as a result, He gave me so much pleasure in seeing the kids growing and learning. His promise to me removed any fear that the radical life we were called to live would mess up the kids' lives. He has been totally faithful to His promise. The kids are all at a peak now in their different careers and life skills, and it's all due to Him.

God did indeed lead them individually and teach them what they each needed to know. I am reminded of the verses from Lamentations 3:22–23: "The faithful love of the LORD never ends! His mercies never cease. Great is his faithfulness; his mercies begin afresh each morning."

I have seen the mercies and faithfulness of God poured out in all our lives, and because we lived life so closely to Him, our kids witnessed firsthand God's goodness and provision. It literally set the course of their lives in directions I never dreamed of.

CHAPTER ELEVEN

MY DEAR LIBBY

The darkest nights produce the brightest stars.
John Green

And [God] calls them each by name.
Psalm 147:4 NIV

Given the fact that I have raised seven children and now have thirteen grandchildren (I imagine there are even more to come!), I feel extremely blessed to have years of wonderful, adventurous, and fun memories to cherish. I'm led to believe that, by the grace of God and my good husband, who was and is an excellent father, I have done some parenting things right. Being a mum has been my calling, and I've seen God's hand on my life as well as on all my children's lives—and I don't take any of those special memories for granted.

But even with all the good and glorious times I've had raising and teaching them, I would be remiss to give the illusion that I did a perfect job. Every mum has regrets she wishes she could go back and do over. That's because we cannot live in relationship with others without sometimes making mistakes or being hurt or misunderstood. Even in the best of families who have the best of intentions, there will still be hurt—it is a given.

I want to tell the story of some of my failures and God's goodness and redemption. If this part of my story helps keep even one other mum from making some of the same mistakes, then it is worth it to me to share honestly from my heart.

* * *

When I was ready to give birth to Libby, we had just finished celebrating our first Christmas in the States, and Rebecca, who was fourteen, came to me, and said, "Can I pretend that the baby is my baby?"

Well, at that point, I thought, *Of course! Any help I can get would be great!* I was touched that she wanted to walk this journey of a new baby so closely with me. And I said yes, not knowing what it would mean or how seriously Rebecca would take her offer. I was just glad to have the help.

So, when it came time to deliver, Rebecca stayed with me through the whole process. She had not watched any birth videos, but as I stated earlier, I was able to tell her what was going to happen so she wouldn't freak out. She was amazed at how everything happened just as I said it would. I had not had an ultrasound, so I didn't know if I was carrying another boy or a little girl, and we were very excited to find that it was a girl! David and I had decided that if it was a girl, we'd name her Elizabeth but call her Libby for short.

After Rebecca got over the excitement that she had a little sister, she asked if Libby could sleep in her room so that she could get up with her during the night and bring her to me for feeding, and I said yes. Rebecca loved changing her diapers, burping her after feeding, and putting her down to sleep again. In the months to follow, she and Libby developed a very close relationship. Libby stayed in Rebecca's room for most of the first three to four years of her life. At night Rebecca would sing to her and comfort her. It was very sweet to watch.

I also loved seeing the attention Libby got from her other siblings. Daniel felt very protective of his little sister, and Ben loved carrying her around. Josh was also very protective of her and would teach her how to play with her toys. He became her playmate.

However, by the time Libby was a toddler, Rebecca started getting busy; she was performing more in churches and then got signed and began touring with David. As Rebecca started traveling more, Libby couldn't understand or comprehend what was happening. She just knew that her Rebecca was gone a lot.

One time when Libby was about eighteen months and Rebecca was away with David, I took Libby with me to Target and put her in the shopping cart. Suddenly she started to cry. And I don't mean a little cry, I mean a *wailing, sobbing* cry. I had no idea what on earth was going on and kept saying, "Libby! What's the matter? What's the *matter*?"

Libby just kept saying, "*Bec!* . . . *Bec!*" in between sobs. When she calmed down a little, I heard Whitney Houston singing "I Will Always Love You" over the store's speakers, and suddenly it made sense. That was the song Rebecca used to sing to her, so Libby had totally attached it to the love she had for her sister. It was heartbreaking to see.

Rebecca was sixteen or seventeen by then and naturally starting to do her own thing and working more, especially after she got signed and became busier from all the demands. So there was, of course, much less attention given to Libby, and she had a hard time coming to grips with her sister-mother being gone.

To be honest, up till then, I'd been fairly oblivious to the depth of what was happening. Other than that incident in Target, which I remember so well, I didn't truly understand the magnitude of the attachment Libby had to Rebecca. I had been so busy myself, I didn't realize just how much Rebecca had done for her.

In the following months, with Rebecca busy, Libby became "all mine," so to speak. And that's when she started to run away. The first time she left, it was around five thirty or six o'clock in the evening during the witching hour many mums go through—the kids are tired, you're running baths, and you're trying to cook dinner. Suddenly there was a knock on the front door, and when I opened it, a woman said, "Is this your little girl?"

I looked down in shock. Libby had left the house and literally walked down the street by herself!

I am embarrassed to say this, but it was only the first of several more times that someone would find Libby by herself down near the road, which was fairly busy. At one point, a lady found her and took her to a house across the street, asking if Libby was her baby, and the woman who lived there said, "No, but the family over there has lots of kids at home, so you might try there." That's how we were known: the house with a lot of kids.

I still had not put Libby's bond with Rebecca in its proper place, and I was confused as to why she would run away. It wasn't until more recently that I actually put two and two together and it began to make sense. Libby leaving the house showed the depth of abandonment she'd had in those days but was too young to articulate. And to be even more honest, she was also a little lost in the family as well. As I've said previously, the boys had one another, and even though we all loved Libby desperately, she found

145

it hard to find her place within the family dynamics—she is very sensitive, and we are a lot of strong personalities.

Life on the road was also a little difficult for Libby and me. She was independent and not afraid to randomly wander off. We would all be busy setting up or running an event, and then I'd look up and say, "Where's Libby?" There were multiple times I found myself panicked and praying while frantically walking around a packed venue looking for her. At one point when we were on the road and in some small town, I actually lost her in a shop in a mall. It scared the daylights out of me, but the good news is it also scared the daylights out of her. After that, she didn't wander off anymore. She actually even reverted a bit and needed to know where people were. Nonetheless, she had a very independent spirit, and I am to this day so very thankful that God protected her.

When Libby was six, Rebecca was twenty-two and at the beginning of the height of her career, and Libby still wanted Rebecca's attention and struggled with how to get it. She would see Rebecca at the merchandise area after each concert with a line of people—some even her own age—being handed a photo of Rebecca and waiting their turn to get her autograph. Libby couldn't figure out why they were in a line for her sister, so she would ask for a picture and get in the signing line too. Rebecca came to me later very confused and saying how awkward it was to see her sister in the signing line. She asked how she should handle it, but I didn't understand where Libby's actions were coming from, so I said it was very important to Libby to be treated like the other people. Libby didn't do this at every event, but it was a fairly repeated occurrence that she eventually grew out of. There was obviously a very real struggle for Libby to find herself and come to grips with what was happening to her sister.

Libby and Josh spent more time together while the others were working, which was good. But during the concerts, Josh hung out with his brothers. So Libby would pass the time by finding a "friend" and playing in the merchandise area. It was often sad to watch her have to say goodbye to her new friend each night. This, too, impacted her long term, as she did not develop friendship skills. She could make new friends, but she didn't understand how to maintain and keep them for long periods of time. Friends were here today and gone tomorrow.

It also concerned me that Libby had what I thought was little to no spiritual sensitivity. I find most kids at a young age are receptive to spiritual matters, but not her. If we had any prayer or devotional time either on the road or at home, she would never close her eyes but instead would look all around at everyone else and give this huge sigh. It was an attitude of, "What on earth are we doing? Do we *really* have to do this?" She seemed detached and uninterested—as though a wall or ceiling closed her off, and we couldn't get through.

I finally came to a point where I knew it was time to really seek God about her; I needed Him to reveal to me what was going on in her heart. I struggled to get my head around hers, and I could not understand what I thought were odd occurrences—her disinterest in spiritual matters, her independent spirit that led her to run away, her need to stand in signing lines, and her inability to understand or express emotion.

By that point, I had heard God speak to me a few times when I sought Him hard, so I went to Him in prayer and said, "God, you're gonna have to help me! I do not understand what is going on here; I don't understand some of the choices Libby makes. I can't get inside her head. Please give me something. Help me here. Give me *some* kind of understanding!"

And He gave me yet another word. It was a promise. He said, "At the moment, she's like a closed bud. One day, I will open her into a beautiful flower."

As with the other promises God had given, I knew He would fulfill this one in His time. I knew He held her in the palm of His hand, and that He would grow her. From then on, whenever I was worried about her, I would pray and leave her with God. I've stood on that promise *so* many times since. I've seen her hurt, I've seen her alone or saying goodbye to a new friend that she knows she will never see again. But I've trusted God to care for her.

One thing I loved about Libby was that she brought out the child in Josh. She was the only one who could get him to be and act his real age. She taught him how to play creatively. As I've said, part of his sensitivity in his mid-teen years was that he couldn't handle or trust his own age group because he was so used to working with adults and his older brothers.

Josh also had a fear of being separated from us and not being able to find us. Even at six, when we'd leave him and Libby in a hotel room while we went downstairs to get breakfast, he would wake up and say, "Libby, Libby! Where's Mum? Where's Dad?" And at four, Libby would calm him down: "Josh! They're downstairs getting breakfast!"

Libby and Josh had always been close, but then came a point when Josh had to make a decision: Was he going to be a kid with Libby, or was he going to be one of the boys? Well, of course he wanted to be one of the boys. There was really no choice, and once again, Libby felt rejected. I could see the hurt come over her face each time he chose the boys over her, and it was hard to watch. I could say what I thought were all the right things to comfort her, but her pain went through to her core, and my words just felt like words—I could tell they didn't penetrate into the recesses of her heart.

The abandonment, rejection, and stress of getting lost in the family dynamics went into a very deep place for

Libby, which none of us could ever really get into. Anytime anyone pushed any of those buttons, she'd leave—she abandoned us, in a way. If we were all having some deep discussion and she couldn't make her voice heard—which is hard when there are eight other people who are mostly outspoken—she'd retreat into herself, then get up and leave and find something else to do. This went on for years, and we all became used to this pattern of behavior.

I came to the point where I realized I had made one of my biggest parenting mistakes with Libby: I'd allowed Rebecca to pretend she was her mother, and I'd allowed the other kids to parent her as well. This was a response made from such a large age range—fourteen years—between the oldest and youngest child. In addition, I was tired, and any support I got was warmly received by me—I could do with all the help I could get! Unfortunately, Libby felt she had eight parents and was always being admonished by someone. She felt she could never do anything right, and this led to low self-esteem and isolation.

I have since confessed my poor choices to her, and she has graciously forgiven me. But once I came to this realization, I began to think of how I was the youngest of three brothers, and with Libby being the youngest of five brothers, I also aligned closely with her situation and could relate too well to her position in the family. This made me either overprotect or overcompensate for Libby in my parenting of her—and neither of these scenarios is great. It led to greater criticism of her by her siblings; it really became a catch-22.

Over time, David and I tried to help Libby find her place on the road. When she was about ten, we tried using her on spotlight, but she got discouraged. Then we had her help us with the merchandising, but it soon became obvious her gifts were more creative, so while she gave merchandising a good try, we knew it was not her fit.

In time we saw that, like her siblings, music was a happy place for her. For a few years she went to a home-schooling co-op where she took a music class, and the kids practiced for a performance for the parents at the end of the class. One night when Daniel was over for din-ner, Libby wanted to practice her song. She gave quite an amazing rendition, and at the end of the song, Daniel looked at us and said, "Where did *that* come from?" Not only was the singing great, but she had excellent stage presence. So when she got to about her mid-teens, David and I thought she should try background singing.

Libby was willing and quite keen, but no one else was very excited about it. They were all pretty stressed from their own schedules and felt that if they tried to invest too much in her, it would hurt their relationship with her; they knew she was sensitive, and any kind of criticism, even though constructive, would be hard for her to take. Libby really wanted it to work—she loved singing and performing—but by then we had been touring on and off for ten years, and the older kids did not have the time or patience to take her under their wing to teach her harmonies and give her feedback through rehearsals. They were all weary from working hard for themselves in their own jobs. Rebecca also had bigger audiences and a band, so the conditions were different from when Libby's older siblings had started out. It was hard, and they needed a lot of support, practice, and encouragement from one another. David said they had forgotten what it was like when they began.

After that rejection, Libby gave up trying. As hard as the situation was, I was disappointed, but I also understood the older kids' side. Libby really needed her own thing—something that did not put her in competition with the rest of the family. God, in His goodness, understood that and provided her with another interest. He knew she had a love for animals; being with them seemed to bring her life and give her joy. So at eleven, Libby started horseback riding, and by about twelve, she was given her first horse by a family friend to use at the farm. At fourteen, Rebecca bought Libby her own horse to ride for show jumping.

She still pushed down her hurts, but riding became both her emotional support as well as her way of setting herself apart from the rest of the family. It wasn't in competition with anyone else—it was God's gracious provision for a very active outlet. It became "her" thing. Of course,

I was glad to see some transformation, but unfortunately, being outside with animals and in the bush brought a whole new problem none of us saw coming.

* * *

Libby was about fifteen when I first took her to a doctor. She had started feeling sick, and I couldn't figure out what was wrong. She had general, common symptoms of being incredibly tired, with body aches and pains, headaches, backaches, and mild fevers, but the symptoms didn't go away over time. The doctor performed all of the normal, routine checks, but he didn't find anything wrong. So we went home. We went back to the doctor and home again about every six months for the next few years. All that time, she had the same symptoms, but the doctor couldn't find anything wrong.

Eventually the doctor and nurses started questioning if she might be a hypochondriac and trying to get attention. They'd say, "Are you *sure* she's not pretending her symptoms?" By then, it was hard not to doubt myself as a mum about the reality, and I took on the attitude with her of, "I'm sorry, but we've all heard it. I've taken you to the doctors, they don't find anything, so I can't take you again. You're just gonna have to get up and face it."

So she did—she got up and stopped talking about it. She did what she could on a given day, but I noticed that she went from working at the barn for as long as she wanted to needing to leave earlier because she just couldn't do the work. She needed to go home and rest.

At the beginning of 2011, Libby was about twenty and working part-time at a retail pet store when David and I traveled back to Australia. I was checking out some posts on Facebook when I saw a picture of her with a little black-and-white puppy, and I thought, *Oh no, this doesn't look good!*

At my earliest opportunity I called her to find out what she was doing with a puppy and what the significance of the photo was. Sure enough, a dog breeder had come into the store and shown Libby a litter of papillon puppies and said she'd give Libby a good deal. Well, what animal lover is going to leave without a puppy? And of course, Buckley chose her. He had crawled up in her lap, and she couldn't resist.

This was the second time Libby had chosen an animal without telling us first, so I wasn't too happy about it. But I must say Buckley was adorable—*and* a handful, like all puppies. Most important, he made Libby feel so loved, and Libby had her very own friend. He followed her everywhere and just wanted to be with her. God knew she needed him for what was to come, and Libby knew she needed him too.

After Libby finished out the school year, she had the opportunity to work at a summer camp in the equine department. This was a Christian camp, and David and

I felt it would be a great experience for her working in a Christian environment with her peers with one of her loves: horses. She signed on for nine weeks.

At the camp, Libby was required to work long hours in the hot sun, and she started to really struggle. She knew she had a commitment, so she kept pushing herself, but she couldn't keep up with the responsibilities. She began throwing up, she got even more headaches, and she began to go in and out of the nurse's station regularly. At one point she came home pretty overwhelmed but then went back to fulfill the commitment she'd made.

Then she started getting sciatic pain shooting down her leg and could hardly walk. By then, David and I knew there was something really, really wrong and she needed to come home and go back to a doctor. The attitude of the camp staff was that she had signed up for nine weeks, so she should complete her time—she still had two weeks before finishing. But she was spending more time at the nurse's station than working, plus she was obviously getting worse, so David offered to pay whomever he needed to in order to replace her. Once they saw his commitment at getting her home, they released her.

My thinking was that since she had sciatic pain, maybe her back was out. So I took her to a chiropractor and booked a massage afterward. The chiropractor couldn't find anything that would create the sciatic pain; there was no misalignment of the spine. But the woman who gave the massage—*she* is the one who discovered a symptom no one had noticed. She said, "When I worked on her muscles, they trembled. I've never seen this before. They were literally vibrating and trembling under the skin."

Well, the mama bear came out in me—that was physical evidence enough to go back to the doctor and do some extensive blood work tests. It was then that she was finally diagnosed with Lyme disease, which is caused by tick bites. Goodness knows we had a lot of ticks on the farm, but no one made the connection in all that time.

By the time Libby was diagnosed, it was 2012. I looked back over her records to see that her first doctor's appointment had been back in 2006, so that meant she'd had the disease for six or so years. And with the issue being bacterial, it was well and truly entrenched in her body. That being said, I now know she was still very fortunate because—and this is part of God's graciousness—only a small percentage of people are diagnosed with chronic Lyme disease through regular blood tests. The disease can be fairly elusive in its detection and treatment, so I'm incredibly thankful Libby was fortunate to have very strong indicators of Lyme antibodies in her blood.

So then began the battle of healing, and God drew the two of us very close. We started the medical route only to find that many infectious diseases doctors don't think chronic Lyme exists. We then went to doctors who specialized in Lyme disease, and then we rounded off her treatments with going the alternative medicine route.

Through this long, arduous journey, it was hard for Libby to have friends. For about three years she could hardly get out of bed. Some days she would try and would have a shower and start to get dressed only to realize she couldn't do any more—she was already spent! During these very hard days God provided her with a best friend in Buckley. He never left her side through the years of pain. He knew when days were hard for her, and I see now that he was a special messenger sent by God for the assignment of keeping her company and loving on her with the love that God has for each of us.

It's been a long, hard road for Libby, and I don't think anyone lives with chronic illness without realizing that we are made up of not only a physical body but a spiritual and emotional one. When one part isn't right, the rest is affected and suffers.

* * *

As Libby worked on her physical healing, she also began to deal with the emotional pain from her growing-up years. Her counselors acknowledged that part of her pain was rooted back to very early days. My testimony today to anyone who is suffering and who will listen is this: Don't run from dealing from your pain. And deal with the whole person. Don't run from facing the emotional, spiritual, *and* physical symptoms, because they are all intertwined. This is what Libby did, and I so respect her journey and the faithfulness of God in leading and guiding her every step. I've seen Him provide what she needed at just the right time, and I've seen her beautiful smile as a result.

Libby and I have had a lot of deep talks about all that she's gone through, and at one point, I said, "Why didn't you, at sixteen, knowing all that you were pushing down and all that you were suffering, just say, 'To hell with you all—I'm leaving'?"

And she said, "You know, I thought about that, but I knew I would mess up my life more by being away from you guys."

Even though the family was part of the trauma that contributed to a lot of her pain, as an adult, she can now look back and know God used Lyme disease to stop her from messing up her life. He put her flat on her back in bed, so it'd be just the two of them, in order to stop her from messing up her life by making poor choices. And with the amount of pain she carried, she would have made poor choices.

Hers is a journey that's unique, and I wanted to share it because sometimes God takes us on paths we don't want or wouldn't choose for ourselves, but that doesn't mean He isn't working things out for our good in the long run. God put maybe ten years of Libby's life on hold through her illness, but she trusts Him enough now to know He will lead and guide her step by step into who He's created her to be and the purpose He's created her to fulfill. God also used her illness as part of the inspiration behind the song her brothers wrote: "It's Not Over Yet." No matter how dire the circumstances any of us may find ourselves in, God is working. He is not finished. Don't give up.

I'm grateful to say with all sincerity that I have seen the fulfillment of God's promise to me made years ago of the beautiful, bright flower Libby has ever so slowly opened up to be. I've seen God's hand on her, and I know He won't let her go. Her life's not over—it's just beginning.

"It's Not Over Yet"

They are inside your head
You got a voice that says
You won't get past this one
You won't win your freedom

It's like a constant war
And you want to settle that score
But you're bruised and beaten
And you feel defeated

. . .

Game set match
It's time to put it in your past, oh
Feel the winter leavin'

It's redemption season
Long live the young at heart
Cheers to a brand-new start
We're revived and breathing
To live a life of freedom

This goes out to the heaviest heart

Oh, to everyone who's hit their limit
It's not over yet
It's not over yet
And even when you think you're finished
It's not over yet
It's not over yet

Keep on fighting
Out of the dark
Into the light
It's not over
Hope is rising
Never give in
Never give up
It's not over

PART FOUR

FOR KING & COUNTRY

CHAPTER TWELVE

TRANSITION YEARS

There's an opportune time to do things,
a right time for everything on the earth . . .
A right time to hold on and another to let go.
Ecclesiastes 3:1, 6 MSG

I call 2007 to 2012 the transition years because this was a hard season for David. There had been some transition in the family even before then, but it was in this period that things got the most challenging. Most managers in both Christian and a lot of secular music have multiple artists to work with so that when one isn't performing and bringing in income, another one is. But in David's case, he had focused solely on managing Rebecca. Plus they were 50/50 partners, which is also different from many arrangements. Normally, artist/manager relationships are set up with the manager taking 15 to 20 percent off the top of gross, which means that after the manager gets paid, the artist then has to deduct all his or her expenses, then get whatever is left—if there is any.

But this arrangement opens up a conflict of interest. A lot of times, while the manager is making money, the artist isn't. Plus there's minimal motivation on the manager's part to keep expenses down. For example, the manager, at the artist's request, could have three buses on the road and a load of equipment because it doesn't make any difference to him—he's not paying for it. This can lead to the artist not making any money for a long time, because they're paying off their debts and expenses.

So before working with Rebecca, David researched how to make it fair for them both. He didn't want to hurt his relationship with her; he was also her dad. Think of Britney Spears suing her father—it happens all the time with management and their artists because they feel ripped off at the end of the day.

So David researched and read biographies to learn how other people in the business have succeeded—how they got doors to open, how they ran their business, the mistakes they'd made. He learned a lot about what works and what doesn't work for the long term. He looked specifically at artists who had twenty-year-plus relationships with their management and came across an R&B artist. They'd had a very successful artist/manager relationship over a long period, which is rare, and David found they were set up to be a 50/50 split of net. With an arrangement like that, the manager is much more focused on keeping expenses down because he's not going to make any money if he doesn't. So they were both in the business together as equal partners from the get-go, and that's the course David took with Rebecca.

When Rebecca got married, and her husband had a good income, she was ready to stop performing. She said, "I'm done." She was depleted from the years of work and was ready to stop.

This was a challenging situation for David. Since she was his only artist, he needed time to transition and find another one to represent. There was a conflict of interest, and in his mind, she'd gotten the very best from him—everything he had to give—for years, and now he needed her to keep working a little while longer so he could figure something out.

In her mind, she, too, had worked very hard for almost twenty years, and she could see it taking a toll on herself physically and emotionally. Rebecca felt as though she'd been a workhorse, and she just wanted to be done. She was also rejoicing in a new season and wanted to bask in that time with no pressure.

The lines between manager and father became more blurred than ever, and it was a very difficult and tough time in every way.

In the meantime, other family members had reached a point of venturing into their own businesses and moving on. As I mentioned earlier, Ben had come to us and said he was done and wanted to get off the road. His love of videography took him on his own path, and he quickly made quite a good business and definitely found his own niche.

Daniel had always had creative business ideas and had started a small business called MusiChristian, which was an e-commerce site. He was also programming lights for other bands, and while he still programmed the lights for Rebecca's events, Luke was the one who took over running them. When Luke wasn't running the lights, he was playing on a basketball team, so his focus was split between the two.

Then there was Josh, who right before finishing school got a part-time job at Premiere Speakers Bureau. As soon as he graduated, he started there full-time. He had a couple of people working for him who had college degrees— women in their thirties—and there he was in his late teens and early twenties. But I am convinced it was because he was so used to working with adults for so many years that he was mature beyond his years. He managed authors' book tours by overseeing the dates and crowd control at all their events, as well as managed the artists themselves by making sure they had everything they needed. It was undoubtedly his sweet spot and where God wanted to use Him.

Both during and after all these changes were happening, David had been working with Joel in ways that looked a bit worthy of David's time and attention. Joel had come to David back when he was sixteen and doing the Timberlake/NSYNC skits and said he wanted to be an artist, but . . . he did not want to be like his sister or be seen as Rebecca St. James's brother. He wanted his own identity. He didn't want to do Christian music—he wanted to perform in the secular industry. And he wanted to go solo. This led to a journey that also put David between a rock and a hard place: guiding and eventually managing not one son, but two, on a path that was far from straight or narrow, and one that eventually led all three to more than any of them could have imagined.

* * *

"So, you want to be an artist?"

David looked at Joel, who was sixteen, and knew he had talent, so he told Joel to write some songs. He could write them with a songwriter or however he wanted, then David would take a look.

And Joel did.

They weren't the greatest songs, but he did end up performing one with Daniel as a support act for Rebecca. They were called the Rebecca St. James Background Dancers because they were so "out there." Rebecca's music was very rock based, and the two boys egged each other on until their moves became quite outrageous. Daniel would finish one song by climbing on the riser and jumping over the bass player and sliding on his knees to the front of the stage.

Well, David watched the audience when they performed as a duo and saw what a lackluster response they gave, so his attitude was like, *eh* . . . And poor old Joel was told to go back and write more.

Joel had inherited persistence and a "never say die" attitude from his father, and he faithfully continued to write with other songwriters. I think he might have been a little frustrated to be performing with Rebecca, but he stuck with it and continued to graciously serve in his role as stage manager and background singer. He always gave his best while working with Rebecca.

Fast-forward a few years to when Joel would have been about twenty. He had continued to write and perform with Rebecca, and by then Luke was seventeen and about to enter his junior year of high school. Daniel, who is quite the sportsman, came to me and said, "Mum, Luke is very gifted in sports. He has incredible hand-eye coordination—he's really very good. I think he's paid the price for being homeschooled and touring and missing out on team sports. He loves basketball, and I think he should be given the chance to play."

So David and I decided that for his junior year of school, Luke could play basketball. He wouldn't miss a game to do a concert; he would make a full commitment to playing basketball.

Well, in his first game, in the second quarter, Luke tore his ACL. ACLs are our boys' nemeses, so it didn't come as a surprise. Out of five boys, only one has *not* torn his, so we have genetically poor ACLs when it comes to the guys. Of the four who've had surgery, they've had six surgeries total.

So Luke had surgery on his ACL, and during his recovery, he realized that any opportunity he had to play sports at college was gone. So that was it—that door closed for Luke, and he was discouraged.

I remember driving home with him from a doctor's appointment, and he said, "Mum, I just don't know what I'm gonna do with my life. So far, everybody else in the family knew their purpose before they left school, or at least saw God leading them into what their next stage of life might look like, but not me. I don't know where God is taking me, and I feel really vulnerable."

I tried to encourage him. "God is faithful, and He *will* lead you, Luke."

About this time, Joel came back to David still pretty keen about doing a solo gig . . .

* * *

Now, David's had some tough times managing the kids. It's hard to be honest and at the same time not hurt the relationship in any given situation. And David had reached a situation where he had to have a really hard conversation with Joel. He'd listened to Joel's demos, he knew Joel had a dream of doing music on his own, he knew he was talented and had great stage presence and a wealth of experience. But frankly, David knew there was something missing.

David finally went to him and said, "Listen, Joel, I know you've got this dream of doing music and doing it on your own, but I've listened to the demos, and you just don't have it. You're a great performer, you're great at what you do, but you just don't have the voice. When you solo act, you're going up against Justin Timberlake, you're going up against the best in the business, and you just don't have the voice. You're not a solo artist."

But then he said, "But you know what? Your brother Luke has the voice. Why don't you partner with him and do music together? You have the passion. You have the stage presence. You have the performance skills. Luke has the voice. Plus, it would take you out of the Justin Timberlake comparisons and into your own unique category, because you'd be a duo, and there aren't many other duos out there. Why don't you write some songs together and see what happens?"

It was obviously a *very* hard conversation to have, and Joel was quite offended. I remember him coming to me at one point and saying, "Mum, why would God give me the passion but not the voice? It just doesn't make sense. Why wouldn't God have given me the voice as well?"

Well, now we know the reason why: it's because it was never God's plan. But all we knew then was that a solo gig didn't look hopeful for Joel, and Luke didn't have a career in basketball or sports. Both of them were in positions of having to step back, pray, and figure out what they were going to do.

This brings me to think about how, after we moved here to America and in the years since, I've developed a mindset of looking for God in all things. I've learned that doors will close, and you *have* to know it's God shutting them for a reason. A closed door isn't a disaster, it's actually just a redirection.

So my encouragement to Luke and Joel was that if God closed a door, He was going to open another one. It's His way of leading our lives, and our part is to keep submitting the situation to Him and looking for the doors He opens next.

Through David's suggestion, as hard as it was for Joel and Luke to hear, we all know now that God was indeed redirecting their lives for His bigger purpose. But reaching that purpose proved to be filled with new challenges and detours that God not only allowed but also used to refine their skills, build their character, and increase their love for each other.

* * *

After David's heart-to-heart, Joel and Luke decided to give working together a try, but it wasn't easy. Joel is number three and Luke number four of the five boys, and while there was healthy competition between them, especially in sports, they weren't close as brothers. Luke still shared a room with Josh, so they had a closeness. Also, Luke had been taken under Daniel's wing a bit because they had the common interest of sports, plus Daniel taught Luke how to run the lights. So they had more in common.

Joel, on the other hand, had always been closer to his older brother Ben—they were a twosome.

Then there was the issue of such different dispositions in Joel and Luke.

Luke is very laid back and much more easygoing than Joel. Remember, this is the kid I found sitting on the mower with his feet up on the steering wheel while the rest of us were working like crazy to rake the yard. Another time when we were all out working, I looked up to find him chatting away with the neighbor.

Well, right off the bat, Luke had trouble remembering lyrics, let alone writing them, and he wasn't concerned with things that mattered to Joel, who was more quick thinking and fast moving and a perfectionist. He was, and is, always drawn into the finest of detail.

I remember back in 1987 or so when Joel was about three, and David was touring Stryper, an American Christian metal band. Their outfits were pretty wild back then, with black-and-yellow stripes and long manes of hair. They also had fascinating album covers compared to most. There was *The Yellow and Black Attack*, and then they came out with *To Hell with the Devil*—both very visual covers. Since David was getting ready to tour them, we had their albums playing at home, and one day I looked over and saw Joel on his hands and knees crouched over the covers just *staring*. It was as though he was taking in absolutely every detail that he could—he was transfixed. There should be no surprise that he later went on to help Daniel create Rebecca's stage designs from the age of twelve. He became quite the artistic perfectionist in most every way.

So while Luke had a great voice and musicality, it seemed as though Joel felt Luke was more of a burden he had to carry than a partner to work with. They were polar opposites in so many ways, and from my perspective, they were like a married couple from the start! They had very complementary skills, but their personalities couldn't have been more *opposite*, and right away, Joel became frustrated as frustrated can be.

* * *

After this new redirection sank in, Joel and Luke got together and started writing some songs. David approached them and said, "Listen, while Bec's performing, Luke, you can still do the lights, and Joel, you can still manage the stage, but why don't you both open for her? You can do two or three songs as 'Joel and Luke' and see how it goes."

David is an artist-development guy and is pretty good at experimenting and sensing whether something may work, so the boys agreed. Plus, they wouldn't know until they tried.

So they started opening for Rebecca. By then, she was doing SHE Mother/Daughter events, plus she was still doing her purity message.

This went on for a couple of years, and after I watched and saw how the girls in the audience responded to them (they were a couple of good-looking boys!), I went to Joel and said, "Listen, I think you and Luke need to address the purity issue as well, but from a guy's perspective." I thought that for young girls to see these handsome young men taking a stance for remaining pure and waiting until marriage would be powerful. So they added talks about girls and women honoring themselves and understanding their self-worth, and the Priceless movement was born and has continued to be a major message of their concerts.

By then, David could tell the boys were on to something. They had written some pretty good songs and started doing showcases, which gave them a chance to introduce the new pieces and to refine their skills. Showcases are put on at small venues or clubs, and management and other artists invite industry people (producers, writers, record company executives) so they can showcase their music and performance. It was then that a producer named Shaun Shankel took notice. He approached David and said, "Gosh, I see huge potential in them, and I'd love to produce them." So Joel and Luke started writing and working with him.

Shaun introduced the boys to a business associate, Judy Stakee from Warner Chappell Music. She was very supportive and got them a publishing deal that allowed them to release an independent EP called *A Tale of Two Cities*. After continuing to do showcases with little response, the new CEO of Word Records, Mark Bright (who produced Rascal Flatts and Carrie Underwood), heard and loved their music and offered them a deal. Knowing Joel did not want to go into Christian music, Mark suggested they release their music through an imprint label called Squint, to be released with Warner Brothers Music. This brought Joel and Luke to the beginning of realizing their dream.

Those were some pretty good doors opening, and it looked as though David's hunch that the duo was unique was now being recognized as something that might actually succeed. But even though this was an exciting step after working so hard, Joel and Luke were still struggling with their relationship and not really working as a true team. Joel was often frustrated, and Luke just tried to contribute where he could. The boys still had some hills to climb in how they worked together.

Looking back, God clearly had a plan for bringing them together, which is what I love about Him—He doesn't abandon us to ourselves. He sees the root of all issues and lovingly addresses them in ways that make the biggest impact on each of our hearts. In that light, things were about to get interesting.

CHAPTER THIRTEEN

FROM DESERT TO PROMISED LAND

"You're here to be light, bringing out the God-colors in the world. God is not a secret to be kept. We're going public with this, as public as a city on a hill. If I make you light-bearers, you don't think I'm going to hide you under a bucket, do you? I'm putting you on a light stand. Now that I've put you there on a hilltop, on a light stand—shine!"
Matthew 5:14–16 MSG

As soon as the realities of a record deal with Word sank in, and that their duo just might actually work, David told Joel and Luke that before they signed any contract, they all had to work out the financial agreements between them. He suggested the same scenario he'd had with Rebecca, as it had worked very well. If they wanted David's management, which was the presumption, then it meant splitting everything three ways.

But Joel's attitude was, "But *I* do all the work! Luke hardly does anything. I should get the higher percent."

David said, "No, no, no, that's not the way it works. We must have equal foundation right from the beginning. It's gotta be fair to *all* parties."

And Joel said, "Well, the work output isn't fair, so why should the money need to be fair?"

My heart went out to Luke listening to this conversation.

David responded, "If you want a long-standing relationship, if you really want this to work, it has to be financially equal across the board." David had examples to show of long-standing partnerships in the music business—including Rebecca's—so Joel resigned himself to the fact that maybe his father's words were true, and they all agreed to equal thirds.

In the meantime, the boys' writings with Shaun had been what is called a horizontal album. That means it's about relationships with one another, so more secular—which is what Joel wanted—rather than being vertical between us and God. Joel and Luke wrote ten songs, while Mark gave them a good budget to make the album.

When the writing was just about finished, however, things took a turn that no one saw coming: Mark was sacked from Word, and the plans for the album halted. Another redirection!

A new guy named Rod Riley then took over, and he saw there had been about a hundred grand poured into the project, so he wasn't going to let it go. But there was a problem, and he contacted David.

"We have a whole album here with no Christian songs on it, David, but I'm not interested in putting out a secular release on an imprint label. This is Word Records—I manage a *Christian* label. I'm happy to put your guys out there, but they have to write three vertical songs about faith. Then we can move forward."

David then had the unenviable job of going to both Joel and Luke—but especially Joel because of his passion to go secular—and saying, "Hey, your dreams of doing secular music have just come to an end. Word will not put out your album unless you add three new songs about faith." And to be expected, Joel was *really* upset.

"This is ridiculous! We didn't sign up for this. We signed up to do a secular deal—that's what we wrote the album for."

Of course, Luke's attitude put him more on the sidelines while David and Joel had it out.

David finally said to Joel, "Do you want a record deal or not? We've done showcases for every major label, and nobody else is interested in you. If you want to do music, *this* is your opportunity. Otherwise, give it up. Go do something else." It was literally the writing on the wall because Joel, who was then twenty-seven, didn't have anything else to do. He was living hand to mouth and had poured his life into making his dream happen.

So the boys wrote three more songs: "Proof of Your Love," "Busted Heart," and "Middle of Your Heart."

As they wrote, it weighed on Joel that they were still called Joel and Luke, so he feverishly worked to find a new title for them. He went through name after name after name, thinking, "We've *got* to come up with something."

Of course, Luke, in his laid-back state, wasn't really sure what the problem was!

At one point, Joel came up with Austoville—a mix of "Australia to Nashville"—and then All the King's Men and ran it by his producer. The dude said, "No, but you know what, what about For King and Country? You know, when the British went onto the battlefield, they'd yell, 'We're going into battle for king and country!' It was their battle cry."

No one really gelled with it at first. They thought it sounded too country—some even criticized the idea—but as I sat with it for a while, God actually gave me a word about it.

I wrote the boys a letter, but before I sent it to them, I sat down with them and said, "I feel strongly that God has given me a word for you guys with regard to who you are and what He is calling you to do. I wrote it out as well, but I want to speak it to you before I send it.

"God gave me several Bible verses, but there was one from Ephesians 6 where we are called to put on the full armor of God. We're all fighting against the spiritual forces of darkness, and I believe this is God's mantra for you: He is calling you onto a battlefield. For King and Country is to be your name because you're fighting out of love for your King, being Jesus, and out of love for your country, being your fellow man. We are all in a battle against the spiritual forces of darkness, and you will be called to fight against our culture."

I felt *very* strongly that this was God's word for them then, and I still do today. I knew that their mission was to fight against the secularization of the culture and to fight for Jesus and their love for others. And that's how and when for KING & COUNTRY was born. Leading up to the release of their first album, *Crave*, Rebecca, who had been doing a few performances just to bring in some income, said she was done and stepped down.

God's timing was and is incredible to me. And what *really* brings a smile to my face to this day is that the three songs of faith Joel and Luke had to add to the album are the very three songs that launched them into notoriety! They were the radio hits off the entire album!

In spite of this leap of success, Joel and Luke were doing better at working together, but Luke still didn't really know his place or his value. Joel understood Luke had a good voice but had some trouble recognizing his worth and the gifts he brought. God was obviously aware of this, because He orchestrated some circumstances that would finally bring them together the way they needed to be—God wanted a strong foundation for this relationship. Thinking about it reminds me that He is *always* working for our good, even when He doesn't appear to be.

* * *

The previous few years of insecurity had been hard on Luke—not that he complained or talked about it. In June 2010, he married the love of his life, Courtney. (Their wedding is actually where Joel met Moriah, who is now his wife.) Times were hard for them all. They were living off "the smell of an oily rag." Both Joel and Luke's individual taxable incomes were around ten thousand dollars. Luke and Courtney were living in an investment apartment owned by his younger brother Josh, and Joel was still living at home. Daniel gave Joel his first computer, and we gave him his first car, which was a 1988 Oldsmobile.

The boys committed *everything* to the journey they were on, and it was tough. They'd take our fifteen-seater van to do small gigs—Courtney went with them and looked after sponsorship and merchandise—and at different times, they wanted to give up in a way. But David's gut instincts about them were strong. He knew they had something special and unique.

When they started writing their second album, there began to be more of a sense of unity between Joel and Luke. Joel still got frustrated by Luke's laid-back demeanor and forgetting his lyrics—not just to new songs, but even ones he'd sung many times! But Luke was also growing in his ability to perform, and Joel started to respect him more for his musicality and the contributions he made to songwriting. They had started to work out a formula where Luke would start the direction of the song musically as well as lyrically, and then Joel would come in and grow it and finish it. Luke is a better starter and Joel a better finisher.

In July 2013, we all went to Southern California for Joel and Moriah's wedding, which is where she is from. Luke and Courtney had had their first baby, Jude, who was six months old at the time. Luke hadn't been feeling well, but none of us had any idea—he and Courtney were keeping it very much to themselves. The day after the wedding, everyone went to the San Diego Zoo except David and me, and we got a call to tell us Luke had collapsed. When we saw him later, with a more focused eye, it was clear he was not well and looked weak.

Then, a few weeks after all of us got home, we got a call from Courtney saying, "I don't know what to do anymore. Luke refuses to eat because everything passes right through him, which causes pain, so he won't eat."

I said, "Put Luke on the phone."

After he got to the phone, I said, "Luke, if you don't start eating whatever Courtney gives you, you're going to the hospital." Luke had a fear of anything medical from when he was younger, so he started to eat.

At that point, David and I got actively involved. I went to live with them for three weeks to help while Luke was diagnosed with ulcerative colitis. The symptoms were debilitating, and nothing helped to relieve the discomfort. I cooked and cared for Jude, who was not sleeping through the night yet, while Courtney cared for Luke, who was also up multiple times a night.

By then—in just the short period of time from when we'd last seen him—at six foot four he weighed only 129 pounds. He was skin and bones and even weaker than before. He couldn't even hold Jude. When Joel came back from his honeymoon, he was told that Luke was so sick he'd have to come off the road. He continued to see different doctors and try different protocols, but nothing really got the problem under control.

Eventually Luke took the advice of a gastroenterologist who suggested an infusion of a pretty strong drug, and he finally started to see some of his symptoms diminish. But he was still very weak.

In the meantime, Joel's attitude of Luke being more of a burden to work with had slowly transformed into more of an attitude of protectiveness and love. I could see Joel was very concerned for his brother, and that concern was about to be put on full display.

* * *

During the time that Luke was down and unable to work or perform, for KING & COUNTRY had been scheduled to play at a Greg Laurie crusade at Angel Stadium in Anaheim, California, which holds about thirty thousand people. Joel had been performing at smaller venues without Luke for a little while up to that point, but this particular performance would be the biggest audience of their career.

The crazy thing is that even though Luke had missed quite a few concerts, he didn't really know how they were doing shows without him. He didn't know who was covering his parts. He was too weak to even go outside—he basically moved from the bedroom to the couch. The performance at the crusade was the first time Luke would get to see their performance without him because it was going to be livestreamed.

I was still staying at Luke and Courtney's house as this was happening, and while we all sat on the couch together waiting for the show to begin, Joel called Luke to download what he and the band were going to perform and what songs they were going to do. He then said to Luke, "You just gotta get better, Luke. You just *gotta* get better. I don't want to do this alone . . . I need you."

My heart was warmed that Joel's high expectations and the grip on his dream of going solo was beginning to soften into a more loving and realistic view of just how much he needed Luke and just how much God wanted them together.

Well, Joel did the performance while we all watched, and afterward, he went back to Moriah's family's house and called Luke to ask what he thought. They both talked about Luke's observations, then Joel said something very significant.

"I'm up there onstage, I'm on my own, and . . . I just want you to know I missed you being on the stage with me. I did all my moves in the first song, and it all felt so lonely. You just *gotta* get better. I don't wanna do this on my own."

My mother's heart broke. I had one son sitting on the couch unable to walk and another son on the other side of the country realizing his own vulnerability. Joel is a very generous, loving man, and in that moment, all the bravado of wanting this for himself melted away and his eyes were opened. In that moment God did a unique and divine work. He knitted these boys together as a team—different yet complementary! He brought them to a place where each could recognize the other's abilities and gifts and not feel threatened by them. A place where there is give and take, love and understanding. Through what appeared to be a bad situation, God created a solid foundation on which to build His band, and I have every confidence that it will stand strong for whatever He has to entrust to them.

God had them in His hands all along, working and purging to build stronger unity and reliance on each other. Just as the children of Israel went forward, backward, and in circles for forty years, Joel and Luke went backward and forward and sideways time and again for a period of eight years while writing well over a hundred songs and putting their first album together. They got some encouragement with a record deal and David's belief in their abilities, but the journey they took before getting to a point of unification definitely had its ups and downs. At the moment Joel confessed his needs to Luke, the right foundation for for KING & COUNTRY was finally established.

After many hills and valleys, God gave Joel what he thought he wanted—the opportunity to perform solo in front of a large audience—only to find it wasn't what he really wanted or needed. How often does God give us something we think we want, and in the getting of it, we realize, "*Ohhh*, this isn't what I want after all!" Sometimes it takes learning the hard way to truly change our hearts toward Him and sincerely believe that His way and His plan is *so* much better than ours.

After all those years of praying about a solo career, Joel realized he didn't actually want to perform on his own—he needed Luke with him. He recognized that he had been taking Luke's involvement and all that Luke brought to the table for granted. And the moment Joel spoke from his heart, Luke experienced the graciousness of God. Luke knew Joel had always wanted the big numbers of people—like thirty thousand—in attendance. Luke knew that events like Greg Laurie's crusade were everything Joel ever dreamed of doing. And in the end, Joel said, "You gotta get better, you gotta get better." It was in that moment for KING & COUNTRY became a true team—with equal rights and equal positions.

God orchestrated the best scenario possible to impact Joel and Luke, and in looking back, I can't help but think of how God so lovingly worked in Rebecca when she didn't want to do an altar call. He worked in her situation so that she would see with her own eyes the importance of what He was calling her to do. In the same way, He lovingly set up Joel to let him see for himself why God wanted him to work and perform with Luke.

* * *

I'm so glad to say the boys are both working in their sweet spots now. Joel recognizes that he needs the spiritual depth, wisdom, and steadiness of Luke. Luke realizes he needs the passion, the drive, and the perfectionism Joel brings. They're able to sit back and accept each other very openly and honestly; they accept their strengths as well as their weaknesses, and they remain very close. Their "perfect marriage" on earth has become a match made from heaven.

I think of Ecclesiastes 4:12 that says: "A person standing alone can be attacked and defeated, but two can stand back-to-back and conquer. Three are even better, for a triple-braided cord is not easily broken." For KING & COUNTRY actually became a cord of three strands—David, Joel, and Luke entwined into God's plan and purpose for their lives and what He wanted to do through them.

I love that David is one of the three strands, with his wisdom and years of experience. He is the holder of the overall vision; he's the long-term thinker who can and will speak honestly into situations that arise, just as he spoke so honestly in the past to Joel and Luke. He is not easily swayed by the persona and power a stage brings. Joel and Luke know that David has always had their best interests at heart. They trust him and know the love they have for each other binds them closely.

Watching from the sidelines, watching the dynamics of the boys' relationship, watching the tensions between them and David at times . . . all I can do is pray, be a sounding board, and try to speak into their situation in ways that will help. Sometimes that is the most any mum can do with the hope that it is enough, and that where she ends is where God begins His all-consuming power to transform and build in ways beyond our imagination.

I sincerely believe that if the boys had found success any earlier, without that true foundation in place, they would not have handled that success. If David had given in and not insisted on the three of them being equally yoked right from the beginning, I know there would have been dissension. There had to be a reckoning that they were all contributing but in different ways.

Sometimes we think that in relationships everything and everyone should look and act "like me." I know I've said this before, but in the body of Christ, we all have different parts to fill—we look different and we work differently. One isn't more important than the other; all are needed for us to work together in a way that glorifies God. Some of us are hands, some of us are feet. But together we're right, together we're perfect, together we are who God wants us to be. We are always stronger together.

PART FIVE

GOD ISN'T FINISHED

CHAPTER FOURTEEN

IT'S NOT OVER YET

You got me when I was an unformed youth, God,
and taught me everything I know.
Now I'm telling the world your wonders;
I'll keep at it until I'm old and gray.
Psalm 71:17–18 MSG

It is now thirty years from the time that David and I left Australia for the United States. Back then, we had no idea of what was before us. We were just putting one foot in front of the other one day at a time. Little did we know the plans God had for us and the journey He would take us on! But we have seen Him. We have known Him. He has been right beside us, loving us, providing for us, opening and closing doors, and blessing us.

And since then, our family has grown. All except Libby are now married with spouses we love very much. We currently have thirteen grandchildren, which takes our family to twenty-eight members. We are a family that still works together, vacations together, and plays together, and as you can imagine, we have pretty loud, fun, and active celebrations. We can also still be a hard family to be a part of, particularly for the introverts. We definitely aren't perfect by any means—we make mistakes and hurt each other as all families do—but we mostly give love, grace, and acceptance as a general rule. David is a true patriarch, and I am matriarch of the whole rowdy bunch.

As David and I enter our senior years—he in his early seventies and me in my upper sixties—we feel called to new seasons. David has retired from actively going on the road and has surrendered most of the jobs he used to handle at one point or another. He used to drive, tour manage, run merchandise on the road, problem solve, manage the office, and lead devotions before each concert. I don't know how he did it all, because he has now been replaced by at least six people!

Giving up those roles has been an adjustment, to say the least. Transitioning from a 50/50 partnership with Rebecca where he basically made all the decisions to being one of three votes and being able to be voted out has not been easy. He has had more than one pity party where he's said he is too old and just needs to do what everyone else does at his age and retire. But God has dealt with him each time and shown him his irreplaceable role that he now accepts and still works in with passion and drive. He is exactly where God wants him, and that is to be the holder of the vision for for KING & COUNTRY. That vision includes loving on the brokenhearted, working in God's economy, living generously, and pointing people to Jesus. With nearly fifty years of experience and having seen the good, the bad, and the ugly of the music business, he watches for trends where the band—both as individuals and collectively—might be straying from the core mission. This accountability is invaluable and definitely God-breathed. Because David is a partner, a dad, and someone who can't get sacked, he has the freedom to speak honestly, even when what he has to say is not popular, and his experience warrants him the respect he deserves.

Currently the boys' work is released through Curb Records and booked through Jeff Roberts & Associates. Both of these companies are owned by septuagenarians who like and respect David—another "cord of three strands" that is not easily broken! They are strong believers who contribute a wealth of experience and provide support as needed from a vault of wisdom. In a world that is more and more owned by big corporations, having the personal attention of these gentlemen has been a bonus in helping David and the boys on their journey.

I believe God has more doors He is waiting to open for them in the future, and we all covet your prayers. What the boys are doing is not easy, and having performed and ministered now for ten years with very demanding schedules and pressures, they are getting weary. It is a hard business to know how to wisely pace yourself.

David, on a day-by-day basis, finds himself mentoring younger friends and associates. He works with the teams at the record label and the office and with the booking agency to keep them encouraged, coordinated, and steered in the right direction. He researches charts and socials to keep abreast of what is current. He also continues to speak into "life on the road" by joining the boys every three weeks or so. So he is still very active. Work, for David, has never really been work the way most define it—it's more his passion, so he continues to put in long hours. However, he also has the freedom to take off some days or spend time with family as the need arises.

Life for me has not really slowed either. I realized ten years ago that I am passionate about family, especially about mothers. It breaks my heart to see families torn apart—the family is the foundation of culture, and the center point of the family is the mother. She holds everything together. A mother, through her children, impacts the world of tomorrow, and yet her role is not hugely respected by society. It is also not recognized for what it is—the most difficult job on the planet. But while it's the most difficult, it is also the most rewarding and godly role.

About eleven years ago I was asked by a younger mum, Heather Rae Houle, from our local church to participate in a mother's mentoring group that met once a week, so I did—and I have been mentoring ever since. Then, about five years ago, through some local circumstances, God challenged Heather and me to use the same model from our local group and take it wider, and we did. We call our model MUMlife Community. The mum in MUMlife is an acronym for "mothers uplifting mothers." It is based on Titus 2, which has the older mothers coming alongside the younger mums to encourage them on their journeys.

At a social dinner about a year ago, a business associate of David's—Rahny Taylor from AccessMore—looked directly at me and said, "How do I get you to do a podcast?"

My answer was, "You don't."

He came back again and said, "I am serious. Families out there are really struggling, and they need to hear from you as an encouragement."

Well, his words started to resonate with my heart and the passion God had already birthed in me. So this time I answered, "The only way you could get me to do a podcast is if you do it with an organization that I am the cofounder of—MUMlife—and that I work with Heather Houle."

He answered, "When can we meet?"

The crazy thing is a month later we recorded our first episode of *MUMlife Community* and have since recorded multiple seasons! Not only that, I love that through AccessMore's global expansion, the podcast can reach and encourage mothers all around the world. Only God!

I feel quite stretched by God in doing the podcast, because I have always loved being behind the scenes. I'm definitely not a front person; it has been fine for me to push the *kids* out into the limelight while I stay safely ensconced in my safe, comfortable environment. But God doesn't want any of us to stay in our safe zone, including me. He wants us to continue to grow and live out our lives—that means our *entire* lives—for His purposes. I know He understands and has compassion on the struggle of being stretched, because I have seen Him lead me gently—first in speaking at our local MUMlife groups, then widening that to the opportunity of cohosting the podcast—and I am grateful.

I have also known deep down for a long time that a book needed to be written about our family story, and I knew it was me who needed to write it. As I contemplated the thought, I knew I wanted to share not just our story but how amazing God is in our story. It all starts and ends with Him. After praying for the right time to actually do it, I felt the nudge about a year ago that the time was ripe.

In addition to writing this book, He has also been pushing me into doing more speaking, but I must say I find it daunting. I don't even want to think about what it means to publicize my book! I have so enjoyed remaining anonymous and unrecognized, and I'm afraid that comfortable space is disappearing.

Moving forward, I know God will give me the strength I need to rise to these new endeavors, and I firmly believe that if He has called me to them, then He will be faithful to give me what I need to be obedient. I will simply do what I've always done, and that is take things one day at a time.

When I'm not podcasting or writing, David and the farm have been and will continue to be my happy place. I am surrounded by open fields and the beauty of life, which entails some of my "friends." We have ten horses, of which quite a few are retired. But no matter the age, in my opinion there is nothing quite as magnificent as a horse grazing in a paddock. I also have two donkeys, one of which was given to me by Rebecca for my fiftieth birthday. I love my donkeys! And then I have six goats, two pigs, and six alpacas.

My latest love, however, has been the introduction of birds to the farm. Libby has been my partner in crime in setting up our own ecosystem with guineas, chickens, ducks, and geese. It's a venture that's been both fun and rewarding, but one of the biggest surprises in it all is how much David loves the birds. Most evenings, he can be found outside putting the birds to bed! And as you can imagine, the farm is a grandkid's delight, so watching them play and explore the same way their parents did when they were growing up is an added blessing.

* * *

After reading this far into my story, you no doubt know about my faith and the journey God has led me on. But I obviously don't know where you are on your journey or where you stand with God. You may recognize that God or a higher power exists; you may have an idea of church, or maybe you've even grown up in church; you may view Christianity as a set of rules or as just another religion; or you may know Jesus. I want you to know that no matter what you think or believe, Jesus loves you and wants a living and active relationship with you where He walks each day with you and literally becomes your best friend! It is the most wonderful relationship you will have in your lifetime. All you have to do is ask Him.

I also want to encourage you to trust your agenda to Jesus. I feel so many of us determine our own steps and follow our own plans, not realizing that God has a better plan for us. We are happy to take Him on *our* journey and ask Him to bless our path. God knows this is a weakness of human nature, as there are so many Bible verses that address this. One of my favorite life verses is from Proverbs 3:5–6: "Trust GOD from the bottom of your heart; don't try to figure out everything on your own. Listen for GOD's voice in everything you do, everywhere you go; he's the one who will keep you on track" (MSG).

Always remember: God not only has a plan for your life but also a purpose. It doesn't matter what age you are. You may be in the prime of youth, or you may be older like David and me. If you still have breath in your lungs, then God is not finished with you—you have meaningful contributions to make in your family, in your church, and in the community.

David and I have taken seriously to praying every day for each of our seven adult children, their spouses, and all our grandchildren. It's been a special time together. We catch up with each other about our day and any prayer needs that may have come from it, then we rotate in praying for the family, extended family, and friends. It is such a special time for us, and I feel we are actively supporting our family for the unique work God has for each of them.

This is actually a legacy gift that I believe both my parents and David's mum gave to us. I knew the value of their prayers for us during our active years, particularly when we were crisscrossing the US in our motor homes. The number of miles we traveled without a professional driver and without any major mishaps or accidents is a God miracle. I know His angels were surrounding us.

I remember one incident in particular that could have been catastrophic, but God clearly spared us. We were traveling through Idaho in winter, and we were driving on an elevated road through a snowy valley. The normal two-lane road was icy on the edges, but in the middle there were two tracks in the snow made by other vehicles that we could follow. Fortunately, there was minimal traffic, so we didn't have to leave the safety of those two tracks very often.

At one point, David was on the phone and the kids were all resting in various places. I had just gotten up to make lunch for everyone when I felt a gust of wind come across the valley and literally push the motor home sideways off the tracks. I saw David drop the phone and grab the steering wheel as I screamed and dropped to the floor, anticipating the motor home falling over the edge—only to realize it didn't happen! I knew in that moment that God's angels had pushed the motor home back on the road. And I felt in my spirit this was a direct answer to the prayers of the faithful—our parents. I am and will always be so very thankful for the godly heritage that we have been blessed with. So David and me now being able to pray for our family is such a privilege.

Sometimes each of us gets so caught up with the day-to-day of life we forget we have a purpose to fulfill, which is the plan God has for us. In our distractions, it's easy to forget we are in a spiritual battle with unseen forces surrounding us. We can forget life is not about us, but rather we are a small part of a much bigger picture we will not see until we sit with Him in heaven. It is all very exciting.

I want to challenge you to live outside the box you may have put around your life. Don't be afraid to look different from society's norm. Have courage to step out and take hold of the dream God has placed in your heart and trust Him. Romans 12:1–2 sums it up so very well:

> So here's what I want you to do, God helping you: Take your everyday, ordinary life—your sleeping, eating, going-to-work, and walking-around life— and place it before God as an offering. Embracing what God does for you is the best thing you can do for him. Don't become so well-adjusted to your culture that you fit into it without even thinking. Instead, fix your attention on God. You'll be changed from the inside out. Readily recognize what he wants from you, and quickly respond to it. Unlike the culture around you, always dragging you down to its level of immaturity, God brings the best out of you, develops well-formed maturity in you. (MSG)

Live an extraordinary life where you see God actively leading you and trust Him for your tomorrow, where you listen to the leading of His voice, where you leave a legacy of faith for the next generation, where you serve Him with your whole heart. The rewards of walking life hand in hand with Jesus are *immense* here on earth as well as in the world to come.

CHAPTER FIFTEEN

WHERE THEY ARE NOW

Direct your children onto the right path,
and when they are older, they will not leave it.
Proverbs 22:6

As I write this update on where all the children are in their lives now, David and I are on a plane to Orlando to attend a couple of concerts in Florida. We try and go out on the road every few weeks, as it makes sense to continue to encourage the boys and the larger team. This is such a good season for both David and me. I love being able to look back on the memories and rest in the understanding that my primary work of being a mother is done. I feel so very blessed! I am proud of who each of the kids have become as they have followed God in their own lives and now with their growing families.

* * *

When Rebecca was growing up as the oldest child of our brood, she said she wanted to beat me and have between eight to ten kids, but her life did not take her in that direction. By the time she turned thirty, she realized that Nashville always reminded her of work, and she had a sense that she was not going to meet her husband there. So with a car full of stuff and a packed trailer, she left Tennessee for California, where she moved to San Diego and shared an apartment with a friend.

She pursued acting lessons and ended up with a few guest appearances in different movies. A year or so after that, she moved up to Manhattan Beach, where she met her husband, Jacob, at a philosophy group. She was introduced by mutual friends. Jacob is a San Diego native and was bass player in a band called Foster the People. At thirty-three, they married. He is the love of her life.

They settled in San Diego where Rebecca enjoyed being a wife. She eventually retired from performing in 2012—the same year Joel and Luke released their first album, *Crave*. Two years later, Rebecca and Jacob's first child, Gemma, was born. Then they went through a winter season between 2015 and 2017 when Rebecca had two miscarriages and Jacob and the band went their separate ways.

In July 2017, the whole family went on a WayFM Thirtieth Anniversary Cruise where both for KING & COUNTRY and Rebecca performed—it was the first time she had performed in five years. The audience was a very safe and intimate group of supporters, and as she performed, she experienced God in a different way onstage than she normally had in the past and realized she had missed it. At the end of the cruise, and on her fortieth birthday, Rebecca and Jacob had a deep conversation about what God had been revealing to each of them separately. They knew He was leading them to Nashville and Rebecca back to singing and speaking. Within two months, they purchased a house in Tennessee and moved. Shortly after the move, Rebecca realized she was pregnant, and Imogen was welcomed into the family in May 2018. They've since completed their family with the birth of River in August 2020.

Rebecca has begun writing and recording another worship album, again with Tedd T., and she has resumed performing. David and I are blessed by the fact that Rebecca and Jacob and their family currently live within a couple of miles from the farm. Rebecca and I catch up over a cup of tea on a regular basis, and the kids are frequent visitors to the farm.

Rebecca's career includes recording ten albums over a twenty-year span. She has more than a dozen published books, she has appeared in eight films including the lead role in both *Sarah's Choice* and *A Strange Brand of Happy*, and she received a Grammy award for her *Pray* album. And . . . she never completed an education beyond the tenth grade. God was faithful to His promise when He told me not to force her to do school and then said He would teach the kids what they needed to know, and He has been faithful to bless Rebecca beyond measure for her commitment and obedience in serving Him as He has led. Living outside the box and following God's paths has allowed her to live in the incredible.

* * *

Daniel has always been a great oldest son. He is very responsible and has set a good standard for his younger brothers to follow. He is known in the family for his generous heart, supporting anyone in need. He worked full-time on the road for years designing and operating Rebecca's lights and staging. He left around 2001 in order to set up and manage a small record company that David wanted to establish called Elevate Records. He also started an e-commerce site called MusiChristian in 2003 and managed the business for seven years until the stress, lack of computer designers, and increased competition forced the business to close in 2010.

He started another company called Lumina Design in 2013 that designs lighting and staging for artists and corporate events, including events for Chick-fil-A and Franklin Graham. He has worked for many major Christian bands and events, including Skillet, MercyMe, Casting Crowns, Chris Tomlin, and Winter Jam.

A few years ago, he wanted to diversify beyond lighting design, and he set up a partnership with a building contractor called Dreamtime Homes. He continues to design and help with new homes and remodels in Nashville.

It was not an easy journey for Daniel to find his lifetime love. He holds the record of having dated more than any member of the family—about twenty years—trying to find his true love. In the summer of 2014 David was accompanying the boys to a concert in Dallas and talking to a ministry friend, Billy Beacham, who jokingly said at the end of the conversation, "I need to set up one of your sons with my daughter."

David replied, "I only have one son left, and that is Daniel."

David followed up with Billy the next day, and both dads researched whether they thought something might work. Unbeknownst to Billy, though, his daughter, Brooke, had just started dating a young man, so meeting and getting to know Daniel was fairly delicate for the two of them for a while. They communicated by email, then texting, and they finally met in person briefly when Daniel went to Dallas the following December. There was no communication for a few weeks, as Brooke realized she had to make a decision between the two guys.

In March, Daniel got a text from Brooke that said, "Mr. Smallbone, what are you doing next weekend?" They started dating, became engaged a few months later, and at the age of thirty-six in 2015, Daniel married his best friend, Brooke.

They lived in Dallas for a while so Brooke could continue her work in financial IT security. Since then, they have moved to Nashville and have been blessed with two children, Isla and Joseph. Daniel continues to design, program, and operate the staging and lighting for for KING & COUNTRY.

* * *

In early 2000, Ben set up his own company called Radiate Films that supplied churches with lyric backgrounds—both still and moving—and with countdowns for the beginning of church. Daniel even bought him his first computer so he could improve his technology capabilities. It was a good small business, but with his incredible eye behind the camera, he became quite outstanding at finding new angles and visuals, and by 2001, he was the first to leave the road. Of all the kids, Ben found touring the hardest—he wanted his own identity, and he also wanted his own friends.

Ben has a crazy imagination and loves the scary and dramatic, and he's always been known as the best storyteller. He loves kids, and they love him. He can always be found where the children are.

Unlike Daniel, Ben found the love of his life early when he met Paige Elrod at our local church. They married in 2005, and Paige has always been Ben's number one supporter. It was not an easy transition for Paige going into such a close-knit family, but she has always been very gracious and loving to us. She definitely paved the way for the other spouses—we were a pretty closed community and proud of our Australian heritage.

Ben and Paige waited to have children because Ben had so enjoyed growing up having cousins of similar age and wanted the same for his children. Paige is now a loyal and loving mother of Asher (2011) and Hayden (2015). The boys continue their father's legacy of love for the outdoors, animals, and adventure. They are creative and have great imaginations.

Ben has written and directed all of for KING & COUNTRY's music videos. He has also worked filming and directing commercials for Chick-fil-A for many years. He continues to hone and grow his skills—he is a research guru and is self-taught. He is another one of the outstanding miracles of our family as God fulfilled His promise of teaching the kids what they need to know. I honestly do not know how he has learned all he knows!

Ben and Joel were both desperate to break into the movie world—they wanted to address the silent industry of human trafficking, which also tied into the boys' Priceless message. They wrote a story, and in 2016 they filmed, directed, and executive produced the *Priceless* movie. It was a huge enterprise that did well, although it did not return what they were hoping. Even so, this film opened even more new opportunities for Ben.

In later years, Ben has been working with Greg Laurie, producing and directing his crusades, both virtually and physically. He has also worked with other artists beyond for KING & COUNTRY, writing and directing music videos as well as a special project with Museum of the Bible and for KING & COUNTRY. Ben has also worked on different films, some in conjunction with the Erwin Brothers / Kingdom Story Company. And he is currently working on multiple films that will be released worldwide over the next few years. Every month his opportunities are expanding.

* * *

Joel is the middle boy and the middle child. I have always been impressed that we managed to raise Joel without him either majorly hurting himself or even killing himself! He has had some close calls! He is passionate and impetuous. He acts first, then thinks later.

Joel is now a ten-year veteran as a recording artist. He takes after both of my parents with a bit of his father thrown in for good measure. My mother could do anything and do it well. Mum had a good mix of creative and dramatic as well as practical, and these traits well describe Joel. He gets his persistence and a "never say die" attitude from his father, and his perfectionism comes from my father. He is a very hard worker.

I think we managed to keep Joel out of mischief by keeping him very busy in his formative years. Of all the kids, he is the one I am most happy that we chose to homeschool—he would not have done well in public or even private school. Joel's strong apprenticeship with Rebecca set him up to win in whatever he applies himself to. He has great marketing and promotional skills and great attention to the smallest of details. His capacity is quite incredible.

Joel met his wife, Moriah Peters, at Luke and Courtney's wedding in 2010. It was really a setup where Moriah came to the wedding as a plus-one to a mutual friend, Wendi Green. Wendi had specifically told Moriah about Joel and felt they needed to meet.

Moriah is a California girl who came to Nashville after she left school to establish a music career and stayed with the Green family for a while. She was signed by Provident Records, but as we saw with Rebecca and other young female artists, the Christian music business is very hard on women, including Moriah. She came as a young, talented, and beautiful teenager, but unlike Rebecca was left alone too much, and it overwhelmed her in a short span of time. It was crushing to watch.

Moriah was not expecting to marry until she had established a career, but as we all know, life doesn't always go as planned. There is an eight-year age difference between Joel and Moriah, and as their friendship grew,

Joel knew he wanted to marry this lovely lady. So they came to a crossroads and decided on a month of silence where each was to seek God and determine what the future held for them.

As the New Year of 2013 opened, for KING & COUNTRY found themselves in Los Angeles for *The Tonight Show with Jay Leno*. Joel got a message from Moriah that she wanted to meet with him postshow. She had decided! She had missed Joel incredibly and knew that she was prepared to take the next step and marry him. They got engaged in February in Nashville at the same venue where they met, and then they were married in California in July 2013. All a bit of a whirlwind!

Moriah has completed a marketing and business degree from Lipscomb University and continues to write, produce, and market her music. She and Joel have for the last couple of years designed and dreamed of their forever home, which sits on the top of a hill near the farm. It is nearing the date of completion, and I know it will be such a blessing to their lives.

* * *

Luke is a gentle soul who has a strong heart for God and for people. He has always been a very natural sportsman and loves the outdoors. From when he was a toddler, he has also loved to mow. It is still a favorite activity, only now he can be found on his zero-turn mower mowing his yard of about sixteen acres. He has done a similar thing to David and me in that when he could afford to, he purchased a farmhouse on a small acreage south of Nashville. He has since expanded the farm by investing in some extra acreage and a small herd of cattle.

His family is his delight. He met his wife, Courtney Helm, at a fairly young age and married in 2010 when they were both in their early twenties. Courtney was not even sure if she would ever marry, as she had a dangerous and rare, often fatal, disease that at eighteen nearly killed her. She spent six weeks in the hospital and had to work hard to build up her immunity and health. Luke walked the latter days of her illness with her, then asked her to marry him after she was given an all clear from the doctors. The disease was now history, and she could move forward in confidence.

They have experienced more tough trials than most people I know, but God has used those trials to grow them and cement their love for Him and for each other. And He has done a beautiful work—their lives are evidence of James 1:2–4 that says, "Consider it a sheer gift, friends, when tests and challenges come at you from all sides. You know that under pressure, your faith-life is forced into the open and shows its true colors. So don't try to get out of anything prematurely. Let it do its work so you become mature and well-developed, not deficient in any way" (MSG).

As we have already discussed, Luke had his own health crisis three years after Courtney's—six months after their first son, Jude, was born and after they bought their first home. He is now stable but has infusions every couple of months. They have had three more children—Phoenix (2014), Leo (2017), and Evie Joy (2021). They are very blessed with a delightful family.

While Courtney was pregnant with Phoenix, she had a lot of sickness and was prescribed an anti-nausea drug. After a few months of using the drug, both she and Luke realized she had become addicted to it. One day, Luke received a desperate call from her and left the road to fly home to help her. She did a cold-turkey withdrawal at seven months pregnant and then a two-week stint in rehab. They have both been outspoken about this dark season of their life in order to help and give testimony to others about overcoming difficult seasons. The song "Burn the Ships" was written directly to the issue of addiction.

The next difficult season for them came two months after their son Leo was born. Courtney was prompted by God to go and check him and found him on his stomach not breathing. Thank God Luke was home! She screamed for him to come and call 911, then prayed over her son, commanding God to give him breath, and . . . He did. Leo sputtered and took a breath. They were rushed to Vanderbilt, and everything was found to be okay except he had a fused skull that was repaired six months later.

Luke wrote "Need You More" from this experience. Leo is truly a miracle baby! Luke and Courtney are reminded of God's goodness every time they look at him.

Before they were blessed with the miracle of their daughter Evie Joy, they experienced a miscarriage in 2019. Anyone who has experienced this loss knows what a hard time it is. When seasons of loss come into our lives, we realize more strongly than ever how beautiful heaven will be when we are reunited with those we love.

God has not only redeemed Luke and Courtney's pain, but He also allowed two songs to be birthed directly from these hard times as well as give inspiration for others. That music lives on to provide encouragement to others in times of their pain. The exponential healing and encouragement that God has given to others from these songs will only be realized on the other side. To Him all praise!

* * *

Now I'm at son number five—Josh. When he was born, I realized that David was the third-generation David Smallbone. I knew we had to continue the tradition, so we named our son David Joshua. He is proud that he is the fourth-generation David Smallbone and the second generation of D. J. Smallbone.

I must say, Josh was a challenging child. He didn't like being separated from the family, so bedtimes became a battle. We often had to literally hold him down in order for him to stay in bed. Then, as a young school student, he would challenge me on why we had to learn things or why we had to learn them a certain way. I got so frustrated that I ended up hiring a tutor, and there were many days she left in tears!

He overthought and worried about a lot of things too. When we traveled as a family in Europe, he would worry about getting disconnected from the group and what he would do. He needed a tour book with addresses of venues, hotels, and contact details for the local promoters. Crazy memories!

Josh started working with Premiere Speakers Bureau before he left school and went on to work full-time thereafter. He managed book release tours with most of the major political and social commentary authors from 2007 to 2015. He developed such a good relationship with Colonel Oliver North that Josh still continues to manage his speaking events. After those years, he joined the team as general manager for for KING & COUNTRY. He has amazing attention to detail, a high capacity for thinking, and he doesn't forget anything.

Josh is also very loyal and knows how to love and love well. He met his wife, Emily Branson, at a young age when they were both in high school. He never had another girlfriend. He allowed Emily the time she needed to complete a degree at Lee University while they continued their growing friendship during her years there.

He traveled to France during her final year at college and carefully planned and prepared a very romantic surprise proposal, and we are very glad she said yes! They married in 2014 and have been blessed with two children, Ronen (2018) and Elea (2020). They are living the adventure!

* * *

Libby continues to be my partner in crime at the farm, encouraging and helping me with the tribe of animals we have all around. It has only been in the last few years that she has been well enough to hold a full-time job working as a veterinary assistant, where she loves the community and the shared love of animals. Healing and fighting for her health has been very hard, demanding work, but she has found her place.

Libby has a delightful personality. She is a creative who loves art, photography, and design. She is the one who designed the shield that represents for KING & COUNTRY. Also, we have a small herd of alpacas on the farm, and she uses the wool to spin and make fiber art. I love how she has brought a cottage industry to life in our home.

Libby has dabbled in writing and singing in the past, and now God is renewing her love of music. He is also currently opening doors for her to write. During her difficult years of healing from Lyme disease, God opened up worship music to encourage her, so she is now actively pursuing worship music of her own.

As the only single member of the family, life can be lonely, but Libby is trusting that, in God's timing, He will lead her to the love of her life. For now, she is happy loving on her pups, Luca and Joy, and working and creating.

* * *

Many years ago, when I was in youth group at my dad's church and we were having different young people stand up to give their testimony in church, I thought about my own testimony. I have grown up in church, I came to faith early in life, I've not rebelled—I've always known God in my life. So when I thought of my own story, I used to think, *How boring!* It was not until years later that I realized I had been given a huge gift.

All of us carry hurts and baggage, but the legacy left to me from my parents enabled me not to have to carry heavy burdens of regret and shame on my shoulders. I appreciate that legacy more today than ever before. I now can see this legacy being lived out in the lives of our children and grandchildren.

I always admired my father for his simple, childlike faith. I once asked him how he could pray for healing for people when he is not sure they will really be healed. He said to me that it is not his responsibility as to whether God chooses to heal the person, it is his responsibility to pray. He loved people and counted it a privilege to pray for others.

So, I dedicate this book to my father. He spent forty-six years in active ministry. Both Mum and Dad got to see his legacy of ministry lived in Rebecca's heart and life. By 2007 my mother died, and in 2011, my dad passed. David's father died in August 1993 before we had a breakthrough in our life here in America. David's mother, at ninety-five years, is still living and has been able to witness both Rebecca's and for KING & COUNTRY's ministries.

When Dad was still living, we encouraged him to see how he had passed the baton of faith to David and me, then to Rebecca, who has since passed it to all of her brothers. And now, with thirteen grandchildren, it will be fascinating to see where the legacy of faith and ministry goes from here. God only knows.

We are not to live our lives in isolation. What we do and who we are will affect those around us, especially the ones we love the most. I encourage you to seek God, grow in Him, follow Him, trust Him. Tell your story of God's faithfulness in your life. Leave a legacy of faith for your family . . .

> for I will speak to you in a parable.
> I will teach you hidden lessons from our past—
>   stories we have heard and known,
>   stories our ancestors handed down to us.
> We will not hide these truths from our children;
>   we will tell the next generation

about the glorious deeds of the Lord,
  about his power and his mighty wonders.
                              —Psalm 78:2–4

Great is the Lord! He is most worthy of praise!
  No one can measure his greatness.

Let each generation tell its children of your
    mighty acts;
    let them proclaim your power.
I will meditate on your majestic, glorious splendor
    and your wonderful miracles.
Your awe-inspiring deeds will be on every tongue;
    I will proclaim your greatness.
Everyone will share the story of your wonderful
    goodness;
    they will sing with joy about your righteousness.
                              —Psalm 145:3–7

But the love of the Lord remains forever
    with those who fear him.
His salvation extends to the children's children
    of those who are faithful to his covenant,
    of those who obey his commandments!
                              —Psalm 103:17–18

And now I leave you with a favorite benediction my father would speak over us at the end of each service: "The LORD bless you and keep you; the LORD make his face shine on you and be gracious to you; the LORD turn his face toward you and give you peace" (Numbers 6:24–26 NIV).

Afterword

Folks have been talking to Helen about writing a book for donkey's years, so it was quite a surprise that, out of nowhere, Helen came to me in 2020 and said that at the prompting of our son, Ben, she was going to write a book and could I find a publisher. I was all ears as I'd started my involvement with the entertainment world by working for a book publisher down under some fifty-two years ago. Little did I know, the first agent I approached, Dave Schroeder from K-LOVE Books, was interested, and within a month we were working on an agreement.

The crazy thing about our life looking back is that we've been allowed to live in the miraculous, starting from when I first met Helen some fifty years ago, a day I fondly remember as the best day of my life.

In thinking through our life together, that's the thing that keeps coming back—the wonder of living in the miraculous. It was pretty average the first fourteen years of our life together. Quite a normal life (if it's ever normal in music): suburban living, Christian schools for the kids, and traditional church attendance.

Then in 1989, everything was taken away. It was shaking but ended up being the greatest gift ever given to this middle-aged bloke. The big surprise in it all was that Helen was open to going to the United States, even if only initially for two years. What saved me from a nervous breakdown (which tends to run in both sides of the family), was that even though for the first couple of years in the US we lived off the smell of an oily rag, Helen never complained. If she had, I think it would have knocked me over.

To this day, I'm thankful to Helen for loving on me then when I felt like a failure. She's the hero in this whole adventure, and every day I find myself thankful to Jesus and this special lady. As a lot of our friends know, I cry when I talk about her (clarification: happy tears). Sidebar, when the going gets tough, and it does for us all at some stage, love on your other half with words and deeds. I've experienced it, and it's given me a wonderful life.

Takeaways from all the crazy things we've experienced:

- Love unconditionally
- Have lots of kids (for us men, they challenge our selfishness)
- Do as much as you can together as a family
- Husbands and wives, pray together every night
- On hard decisions, look for the Jesus answer, not the business answer

- Be in church
- Have accountability partners

In conclusion in this little epistle: Has life been perfect? No. Has it been wonderful? Absolutely.

Thanks very much for reading Helen's book.

Final challenge: find a way in every conversation you have to involve Jesus, even if in only one sentence. At my vintage, threescore and twelve, I've realized life is short. Do the world a favor, share the hope in Jesus with whomever you can. If you are not a Jesus follower, start following him now. You'll never regret it!

Blessings to you and yours,
David Smallbone

Acknowledgments

It has been thirty years since we came to the United States and our new life began. We had no expectation of what life would look like. We just stepped forward each day doing what God put in front of us.

Snippets of our story have been told privately as well as publicly, usually by our son Luke, who incorporates it as part of his Compassion sponsorship talk. Over the years when people hear the snippets, they make the comment "You have to write a book one day!" My usual answer is "Yes, one day . . ." In the meantime, I have focused on other things and prayed that God would let me know when the time was right.

In January 2019 a lot of the family, including David and me, returned to Australia for a for KING & COUNTRY Australian tour. A lot of memories were resuscitated, relationships renewed, and details refreshed. It was quite an emotional experience for us to go back and remember. On that Australian tour, for KING & COUNTRY performed two sold-out shows at the Sydney Opera House. Quite staggering to be in that major venue again but over forty years later. Thoughts of a book grew.

Acknowledgments

In the summer of 2020, our son Ben was at the farm filming interviews for a family documentary. I was retelling some stories over a meal and someone at the table said, "You need to write a book." In that moment I realized the time was right. It was as though a switch had been flipped. I mentioned it to my shocked husband, and he made the appropriate calls that have brought me to this place.

I have never had a desire, or even a thought, that I would have any type of public profile other than being someone's mother. However, I have felt God's nudge, encouraging me to venture out of my comfort zone. I am stepping out in obedience not knowing how I am going to do this but trusting He will equip me for the journey He has before me.

Early in 2021 I was given the names of a couple of cowriters. I felt a kindred spirit immediately with one of the writers, Lisa Stilwell, during our interview. Lisa has over twenty years of experience in Christian publishing. It helped that we are in similar life stages as she has three adult children as well as grandchildren. Lisa has experienced some tough seasons that have caused her to grow in her faith and really lean into her relationship with Jesus. However, when I heard her mention that she was stepping into new territory out of obedience to God's call, I knew I had found my cowriter. Lisa has been a true partner in the writing of this book! I have prized our times together as well as her godly wisdom, biblical knowledge, and insight. It has been a pleasure. Thank you, Lisa.

Thank you to K-LOVE/WTA for taking a risk on this novice writer and especially Dave Schroeder for his sweet spirit, active support, and partnership. I know there are many other people involved in this project that I have not met. Thank you for using your gifts to enhance this book. I hope that it has been a blessing to you. Thank you, too, to Matt West and his team at Dexterity for their help in the publishing process.

It has been fifty years since I met my husband, David. He has been my best supporter and encourager throughout our years together. He has believed in my being able to write this book. It is beautiful to grow old with the love of your life who knows you inside out. David is my best friend. I love walking through life with him at my side.

For each of our children, Rebecca, Daniel, Ben, Joel, Luke, Josh, and Libby. You lived this adventure with us. I hope you are okay with the stories I have told about you and that you will again be amazed with the special journey God has given us.

> Don't you see that children are GOD's best gift?
>   the fruit of the womb his generous legacy?
> Like a warrior's fistful of arrows

are the children of a vigorous youth.
Oh, how blessed are you parents,
    with your quivers full of children!

—Psalm 127:3–5 MSG

I am very blessed! Each of you are God's best gift to me. I love being your mum! You have each brought me so much joy. I am very proud of each one of you, proud of the men and women you have become, proud that each of you want to make a difference with your life, serving our Lord and Savior, Jesus.

And that brings me to the One who holds it all together, who offers joy and peace each new day, His faithfulness and His goodness last forever.

But I lavish unfailing love for a thousand generations on those who love me and obey my commands.

—Exodus 20:6

I live in His unfailing love . . . to Him be the glory!

Now all glory to God, who is able, through his mighty power at work within us, to accomplish infinitely more than we might ask or think.

—Ephesians 3:20

About the Authors

Helen Smallbone is the co-founder of MUMlife Community and a podcast host with AccessMore. Her passion is encouraging mothers and families with the God-breathed wisdom she has gleaned over thirty-two years of active mothering. Born and raised in Australia, she dedicated her life to Christ as a young teen at the Billy Graham Crusade in Sydney. Now a mother to seven—five boys, bookended with girls—and grandmother to fourteen, she currently lives outside of Nashville, Tennessee, with her husband, David, and a small menagerie of animals.

Lisa Stilwell is a veteran in Christian publishing with twenty-plus years of experience and is the owner of Loadstone Literary, a comprehensive freelance editorial service that provides book development, editing, and ghostwriting. She's worked with best-selling authors such as Max Lucado, Charles Stanley, and Sarah Young. She is also the author of *God's Truth for Troubled Times* and *100 Days of Faith Over Fear*. When Lisa isn't writing or editing, she loves to be outdoors hiking and kayaking.